BRECHFA AND BEYOND:
The Peregrinations of a Parish Priest

Brechfa and Beyond:

The Peregrinations of a Parish Priest

Patrick Thomas

Published with the financial support
of the Welsh Books Council

ISBN: 978-1-84527-229-6

Cover design: Sian Parri

First published in 2009 by
Gwasg Carreg Gwalch
12 Iard yr Orsaf, Llanrwst, Wales LL26 0EH
tel: 01492 624031
fax: 01492 641502
email: books@carreg-gwalch.co.uk
website: www.carreg-gwalch.co.uk

*This book is dedicated to my wife Helen
and our children Iori, Gareth, Llinos, Mair and Gwenllian,
with much love.*

Acknowledgements

I am grateful to Henry and Frances Jones-Davies, editors of Cambria,
for first publishing the articles contained in this book
and for their kind support over the years.

A profound debt of thanks is owed to Jen Llywelyn of Gwasg Carreg Gwalch
for selecting the articles for this book
and overseeing their publication with such care and thoughtfulness.

I am also extremely grateful to Bishop Wyn Evans for his constant encouragement,
and for providing a foreword to the volume.

The help provided by the staff of the National Library of Wales,
St Deiniol's Residential Library, Hawarden, and Carmarthen Public Library
has been invaluable, as has that of Nona Rees and Debbie Williams,
my colleagues at St Davids Cathedral Library.

Both my present parishioners in Christ Church/Eglwys Crist, Carmarthen
(also known as the Parish of Carmarthen St David) and my former flock in Brechfa,
Abergorlech and Llanfihangel Rhos-y-corn, have shown extraordinary patience
with their increasingly absent-minded 'literary parson'. I am also especially thankful
to my colleagues in ministry, the Reverend Mary Thorley,
the Reverend Dr Simon Oliver, the Reverend Ainsley Griffiths,
the Reverend Leslie Evans, Canon Haydn Rowlands and Mr Michael Kirby,
for their friendship and tolerance.

The translations of Welsh poetry are my own.

Contents

Introduction

I have to admit that the first article to which I turn when my copy of *Cambria* arrives is that by Patrick Thomas. This is not just because he is a friend of long standing and a valued colleague and, as readers of a recent article of his in *Cambria* will know, the Canon Librarian of St David's Cathedral.

It is, and I am sure that the many readers of *Cambria* magazine will agree with me, because his articles are always focused, of a constantly high standard and demonstrating a rare and deep knowledge of so many fields of interest.

The articles selected for this collection make that point eloquently, as they range over the history, mythology, folklore, and literature of Wales. They are seasoned in theology and grounded in a penetrating but kindly observation of the people and landscape of Wales.

It is good that they have been brought together not only so that many of us can renew acquaintance with them but also that they may attract a new audience. Those of us who have, like him, served as country parsons, can and do recognise the characters and the tropes of rural life and the importance of '*y Pethe*' that are the bedrock of the Welsh experience.

It therefore gives me great pleasure to commend this collection to your attention.

Wyn St Davids

Introduction

The phone call came from Libya. Henry Jones-Davies (who normally lives in Nantgaredig, six miles down the road from the rectory in Brechfa) wanted to know if I would contribute an article to a new magazine. The publication would be concerned with Wales, have very high production standards, and its working title was Cambria. I duly produced 2,000 words. More phone calls ensued (and then e-mails, as technology advanced). Often having to meet a tight deadline in the midst of the many demands of parish life, I foraged in the peculiar dustbin of my mind for subjects. Some of the results have been collected together in this book.

My view of Wales comes largely from the patchwork of communities where I have lived for varying lengths of time. Welshpool *(Y Trallwng)* was my birthplace, and the area around it provided my memories of Wales after I crossed Offa's Dyke at the age of seven. St Davids *(Tyddewi)* was the scene of a spiritual and cultural awakening when I went on holiday there as an undergraduate. That gave me the impetus to study medieval Welsh under the wise guidance of Dr Rachel Bromwich on my return to Cambridge. It also started me on a rather tortuous journey of faith that ended in my returning to the Cathedral in Dewisland to be ordained. Before that I had come back to Wales, burying myself in seventeenth century poetic manuscripts in the National Library in Aberystwyth, desperately but unsuccessfully attempting to escape my vocation to the priesthood. Ironically enough, after theological training, I returned to Aberystwyth to serve my first curacy under George Noakes, who taught me to love the Welsh language as much as my mother tongue.

It was, however, during the seventeen years I spent in the north Carmarthenshire parishes of Brechfa, Abergorlech and Llanfihangel Rhos-y-corn (a forest, a valley and a mountain) that I stumbled across genuine Cymreictod: a sense of belonging to a place and its people with a deep-rooted and unique culture – even if, tragically, much of that culture was facing terrible pressures and the threat of being eroded completely. Brechfa possessed a glorious eccentricity and a very special character which, I hope, emerges from several of the articles in this collection.

Other pieces reflect occasional or lasting enthusiasms. The traditions linked to the sixth century 'Age of Saints' in Wales have helped to shape my personal spirituality. A deep-seated loyalty to Montgomeryshire passed on by my father explains the essays connected with that area. The reflection on Llywelyn ap Gruffudd stemmed from an invitation to speak at Abaty Cwm-hir on the anniversary of his death. Many years of family holidays in Aberdyfi made me think about *Cantre'r Gwaelod*, while my wife and I did much of our courting in the area around Llanbadarn Fawr, which is associated with Dafydd ap Gwilym's love life.

Welsh-speaking Anglicanism has been an enthusiasm and inspiration throughout my ministry. The article about the struggle for a Welsh-speaking episcopacy came partly from my surprising discovery, as an ordinand at theological college in Yorkshire, that most of the churches that I preached in had been built by exiled Welsh clergy, and also from an invitation to give a lecture to Cymdeithas Carnhuanawc in the Meifod National Eisteddfod. Welsh-language Anglican folk theology is best enshrined in the carols composed by Vicar Prichard and his successors. A short sabbatical provided by a thoughtful bishop enabled me to produce the studies of carols and their background contained in this volume. My latest and most improbable obsession (with the Armenian cultural and spiritual tradition) has left its mark on one essay in particular.

In the nineteenth century *'personiaid llengar'* made a major contribution to the survival of a great many important Welsh cultural institutions. The handful of clerics who fall into that category at the beginning of the twenty-first century may seem to be an eccentric anachronism. For me, however, a love of Wales, her culture and her people has always been inextricably intertwined with the love of learning and the love of God. If something of the extraordinary delight that flows from that combination is sensed by some of those who browse in this book, the effort will have been worthwhile.

Patrick Thomas
Caerfyrddin

Confessions of a Canon Librarian

(Summer 2008)

Dean Wyn Evans emerged from his vestry in St David's Cathedral with a characteristic twinkle in his eye. "You can read and write, Patrick," he said affably. "You'd better be Canon Librarian from now on." I accepted with quiet enthusiasm. The words 'Canon Librarian' conjured up a musty, be-cobwebbed figure from an M.R. James ghost story, emerging in his clerical frock coat from behind a bookcase of massive leather-bound folios. The reality was more prosaic. The title turned out to be largely honorary, any hard work actually being done by Nona Rees, the energetic, efficient and highly effective Cathedral Sub-Librarian.

The Cathedral Library is in a suitable setting, only reached by climbing a stone spiral staircase. It has a respectable share of hefty theological tomes, several delightful surprises an impressive collection of material concerning the Cathedral and the St David's area. Sadly, most of the really good stuff was either destroyed by over-zealous sixteenth-century Reformers, or looted by Oliver Cromwell and given to Trinity College, Dublin. Although my Irish grandfather went to Trinity Dublin, the Welsh side of me suggests that we should be mounting a campaign to get some of it back.

Despite such depredations, the Cathedral Library still looks like a genuine library (rather than an Information Retrieval Centre). Interestingly enough that is what seems to make the greatest impression on those visitors who venture up the spiral staircase. The 'book-less library' with its row of computer screens may help to remove the constant pressure to find storage space for books, but, for a cheerfully old-fashioned individual like myself, surfing the internet will never have the same attraction as stumbling across some unexpected delight while browsing among the bookshelves.

Not that reading is without its dangers, of course, as I discovered early on in life. One of the first full-length books that I ever read was a volume by Enid Blyton. It contained an intriguing reference to someone having their ears boxed. We were living at Buttington, just outside Welshpool, at the time. My mother, pushing a pram containing my baby sister, took us on a family walk to the village signal-box. She stopped for a moment, and the desire to experiment proved too much for me. I was still quite small, but I managed to lean into the pram and (gently and tentatively) box my sister's ears.

Her howls of woe and my mother's outraged reaction should have warned me off books for ever. Instead my fascination grew. I frequented libraries. My sister and I shared a ticket for the library in Boots the Chemist, taking it in turns to choose books. Hers were either about ponies or sagas of hard-done-by girls who eventually overcame the machinations of evil step-mothers and jealous rivals to emerge, overwhelmed with applause and bouquets, as the surprise stars of royal command ballet performances. It was a relief to gain entrance to the local public library.

At a boarding school on the far side of Offa's Dyke I came across my first really eccentric librarian. J. B. Lawson was an authority on Shropshire local history. He was bald on top, with a whoosh of black hair sticking out at the sides, thick glasses, a pointed nose, a moustache and earnest expression. He speeded around on a racing bicycle with his academic gown flying behind him, and thus, predictably enough, was nicknamed 'Batman' and treated with that ferocious cruelty that teenage boys delight in inflicting on vulnerable teachers.

The school had been founded by Edward VI and had an ancient library that included many early printed volumes and manuscripts (including the medieval Welsh 'Shrewsbury fragment'). On Sunday mornings, after the somewhat dreary ritual of compulsory school chapel, Mr Lawson would guide the handful of us who were interested through some of the treasures in his care. I still remember the intriguing woodcuts from one of the oldest books: the massive and fascinating Nuremberg Chronicle.

Arriving in Cambridge, the college librarian was an astronomer named Dr Shakeshaft. He lived on the roof of St Catharine's in some rooms that were rather impressively known as 'Sky Hall'. Neighbouring King's College had abolished 'gate hours', whereas our gates were still locked at a certain time, with potentially severe penalties for latecomers. Those who did not wish to be impaled on the spikes of the college's decorative but lethal wrought-iron railings, would have to venture across the roofs from King's. This was a fairly risky business in itself, but the possibility of being caught in the lens of Dr Shakeshaft's telescope added an extra element of terror.

The University Library was, however, the greatest source of delight. Most of the books were on open shelves and so easily accessible. This meant that, while trying to track down one book, you always came across a score of others of which you were wholly unaware, and which usually proved to be far more interesting. The sheer vastness of the building gave it something of the feel of Jorge Luis Borges' 'Library of Babel' (which contained every possible book).

One afternoon I got hopelessly lost and ended up in the Pali and Sanskrit section. To my horror, I almost tripped over a man's body lying on the floor between the books. He might well have been dead or (given the nature of the volumes around him) deep in some form of exotic meditation. Perhaps he was simply asleep. The University Librarian had attracted some attention shortly before by saying that he preferred readers to sleep in the library, as they did less damage to the books. I suppose I should have tried to test out the various possibilities, but being both disorientated and rather less than heroic, I simply wandered on.

Appalled by my growing sense of religious vocation, I turned my back on God and Cambridge and headed for Aberystwyth: a return to my Welsh roots and the shamefully self-indulgent joy of literary research. For three years the National Library of Wales became my second home. Each day I struggled up Penglais Hill to what, to my mind, is the most beautiful library in the world (with the Matenadaran in Yerevan, Armenia, coming a close second).

Research had its hazards. This was before the days of computer catalogues. As an impoverished scholar I was wearing some trousers that had once belonged to my grandfather, and a belt that was somewhat frayed. In a rash moment I bent down to search among the index cards on the bottom shelf. There was a sudden phtwang as my belt disintegrated. I managed to grab my trousers just in time – but had to make a shamefaced exit with my academic library-cred in ruins.

Attempting to remedy the sartorial challenges of poverty, I got a part-time job in the kitchen of a chip shop in Borth. My chips were so terrible that I was quickly relegated to making tea and washing up. I could now confidently reach into the remotest card index without fear of disaster, as the quality of my clothes had improved. Unfortunately my secondary occupation meant that my jacket was impregnated with the powerful odour of chip fat. Until my finances improved and I was able to abandon the café, my fellow readers tended to avoid the Rare Books Table.

The members of staff of the manuscripts section at the National Library were particularly wonderful. They pointed me in the direction of documents that I otherwise would not have been aware of, and warned me when visiting American scholars were about to 'discover' literary papers that I had been working on for many months.

If the building in Aberystwyth and its contents are national treasures, my experience was that many of those who work there are even more so, combining a depth of scholarship with a cheerful readiness to help those who turn to them for advice.

Perhaps it was inevitable that I should have become engaged to a student from the College of Librarianship of Wales in Llanbadarn. We met on an Anglican Student Society outing to St David's University College, Lampeter. Helen had caught my eye during the service in the college chapel, and I managed to sit next to her at the supper which followed. While pouring her a cup of tea, I noticed that the stainless steel tea pot was empty. There was a matching jug next to it, which I assumed contained hot water. Having poured its contents into the teapot, I filled Helen's cup. Unfortunately the jug contained gravy. Perhaps it was that moment which made her realise that I was in desperate need of someone to look after me. Thirty years later she is still trying to reduce my natural chaos to a semblance of order.

Meanwhile God caught up with me again, and the conviction had dawned that there might be more to life than not very good seventeenth-century poetry. The Diocese of St David's, faced with an acute clergy shortage, decided that it might have some use for me. I was sent off for training to a theological college run by the monks of the Anglican Community of the Resurrection at Mirfield in West Yorkshire. The Community Library was unique. Father Gordon Arkell, a truly eccentric librarian, had classified his enormous stock of books in a delightfully idiosyncratic way: "My own modification of Dewey", as he announced proudly. One factor that played a significant part was his desire to shield his brethren from any publications that might lead them astray. Perhaps his greatest achievement was to classify the controversial novel *Portnoy's Complaint* (which is mostly about masturbation) under 'Sociology'. "It's all right," he whispered to me confidentially. "It'll be quite safe there. Monks don't read sociology."

During my first year at theological college I was given the task of cleaning the lavatories – the usual monastic remedy for bringing the over-studious or otherworldly down to earth. Duly chastened, the following year I was put in charge of the two college libraries. The Theological Library was full of substantial works of academic scholarship, while the Devotional Library supposedly contained somewhat lighter spiritual fare to be read during our silent breakfasts. No-one was quite sure how a copy of Hitler's *Mein Kampf* ended up in the Devotional Library. College mythology alleged (no doubt quite slanderously and without foundation) that it had been put there when a particularly ferocious monk, Father Anselm 'Jackboot' Genders, was Principal. Father Anselm was later made a Bishop and despatched to sort out the allegedly errant and decadent Diocese of Bermuda. Many years later I preached at a service in Merthyr Tydfil at which he presided. I was careful not to mention *Mein Kampf*.

Since my ordination at St David's in 1979 much of my ministry has been spent in parishes that are tantalisingly remote from research libraries. On a few occasions, however, I have had an opportunity to stay at one of Wales' most unique and valuable institutions: St Deiniol's Library, Hawarden. This was Mr Gladstone's special legacy to the church and people of Wales. It's a residential library, where visitors can stay in comfort and make use of the extensive collection of books. The food is rather good and the company always interesting, as it attracts a fascinating mix of people from Wales and beyond. It's an excellent place to study and write, or simply to browse and relax. It also seems to have a soothing effect on the clerical soul. An archdeacon who had always terrified me during our occasional encounters at the Governing Body of the Church in Wales, was transformed by Hawarden into a delightful and entertaining table companion.

Libraries are changing fast, and some of the developments are to be welcomed. For example, it's extremely useful to be able to browse through the on-line catalogue of the National Library, e-mail your order for the books you require, and find them waiting ready for you when you trek over to Aberystwyth. Nevertheless, there is still a special enchantment in an old-fashioned Cathedral library, reached by a spiral staircase, in a corner of one of the most sacred places in Wales.

'Raising the heart':
the world of a Welsh country priest

(Autumn 2002)

Welsh rural clergy are by nature very possessive about their territory. Only a very special priest can become a partner and guide to his successor. I was almost uniquely fortunate to be blessed with such a predecessor for my first eight years in the north Carmarthenshire hill parishes of Brechfa, Abergorlech and Llanfihangel Rhos-y-corn. His name was Eric Myrddin Grey and he had been in charge of the three churches from 1960 until 1983. When he retired he assumed that no one would be appointed in his place and so he continued to live in Brechfa. Then, out of the blue, in 1984 I rang him up to say that the bishop had asked me to look around the parishes. He was astonished. *'Ti'n jocan, 'machgen i!'* ('You must be joking, my boy'!), he remarked. But I wasn't.

Not long afterwards I knocked on the door of Llystyn Cottage, Eric's retirement home. A short, round, bespectacled priest with a mischievous twinkle in his eye welcomed me in. As we set out to look at the churches he grabbed a deerstalker from a peg by the back door. It was his favourite headgear. There was a time when canons of the Church in Wales were allowed to wear natty little black rosettes on their hats. An old-fashioned bishop once noticed the deerstalker and asked 'If I were to make you a canon, Grey, where would you put the rosette? 'You make me a canon, my lord,' Eric replied, 'and I'll find somewhere to stick it.' Sadly the bishop didn't take the hint.

Eric Grey had been born in the east Carmarthenshire industrial village of Llandybïe. His forebears had originated in Scotland and come to work in the copper mines in Anglesey before finding their way to West Wales. He was the youngest of a large family and his mother was a remarkable woman whose spiritual life had been indelibly marked by the great religious revival of 1904. Her prayers and self-sacrifice helped to push Eric towards the vocation that led to his training for the priesthood at Lampeter and Lichfield.

The Second World War interrupted his preparation for ordination. The would-be cleric was drafted into the Army Pay Corps and was soon promoted to lance-corporal. Unfortunately the night after he earned his stripe he lost it again for being asleep on guard duty. Eric approached the trials of army life with characteristic humour. Once, as a punishment, he was sent to clean the officers' latrines. He wrote 'Out of Order' on some scraps of paper and pinned one to each of the stalls. As a result the officers suffered far more than Eric did. He ended up at Meerut in India where he arranged a memorable St David's Day dinner for his fellow Welsh servicemen.

After curacies in Aberaeron and Cwmaman Eric became vicar of the Cardiganshire parish of Capel Cynon. It was there that he began to take an interest in politics. A local councillor had died and Eric decided to stand in the by-election. His opponent was the deceased man's son. 'I didn't think the lad stood a chance,' Eric said. 'He didn't have any policies, but just went around asking people to support him for his father's sake. I felt very sorry for him. The night before the poll I knelt down and asked God to give him just a few votes so that he wouldn't be too disappointed. When the result was declared he'd won by a landslide.' Eric's political enthusiasm was not dampened by this defeat. After moving to Brechfa he became Gwynfor Evans' agent and played an energetic part in helping Plaid Cymru win its first ever seat in the Carmarthen by-election of July 1966.

Not long after Eric's arrival in Brechfa a truculent parishioner reported him to the bishop. The new rector was duly summoned to the Bishop's Palace at Abergwili. He was ushered in to face Bishop John Richards, a short but formidable prelate whom his clergy nicknamed 'The Shah', because he had once been Archdeacon of Shiraz in Persia (Iran). Bishop Richards flourished the letter of complaint. 'I wouldn't take it too seriously, my lord,' Eric commented, 'He's an old man, and you know what old men can be like.' 'How old is he?' the bishop asked. 'Seventy-two,' Eric replied. 'And how old do you think I am?' enquired Bishop Richards (who also happened to be seventy-two).

Bishop John Richards's successor was Bishop Eric Roberts. Bishops of St David's sign letters and documents with their Christian name and the name of their see. Eric Grey received a Christmas card from his new bishop signed 'Eric St Davids'. The temptation was too much for him. He sent the bishop a card signed 'Eric Brechfa'. Eric Grey was never one of those smooth and slightly sinister Trollopean clergymen who conspire and flatter their way into ecclesiastical preferment. Any possibility of his ever being promoted to a 'plum parish' was dashed forever when he wrote a witty article in a Welsh language magazine explaining why (in his opinion) the Church of England tended to have more interesting and colourful bishops than the Church in Wales.

He disliked po-faced clerical pomposity. At one diocesan clergy school there was a visiting speaker from the other side of Offa's Dyke who took himself very seriously indeed. 'Whenever I visit a house in my parish,' this man remarked piously 'I always knock three times: in the name of the Father, and of the Son, and of the Holy Ghost.' Some of the clergy were sitting quietly in the common room later in the day when their peace was shattered by a single thunderous knock on the door. It flew open and there was Eric. 'Unitarian!' he announced.

One of the parishes attached to Brechfa was Llanfihangel Rhos-y-corn, a remote depopulated mountain area. When Eric arrived in 1960 it had two churches. One, in the hamlet of Gwernogle, was an *'eglwys shinc'* – a corrugated iron mission church. The other was a simple medieval stone building high up on the mountainside. Both were in an advanced state of dilapidation. Eric sold the eglwys shinc to the local Young Farmers' for a few pounds. He then launched a vigorous campaign to rescue the ancient church on the mountain. Whist Drives played a key part in this. He took posters advertising them wherever he went. One year he ventured to England and visitors to Blenheim Palace were startled to find a large placard attached to the gates inviting them to a Grand Whist Drive in Llanfihangel Rhos-y-corn.

A part of Brechfa's appeal for Eric was the river Cothi. He was a keen fisherman. Wealthy visitors would come from the Home Counties to stay at the Forest Arms in the village. They would assemble their expensive fishing tackle and set off for the river. After many hours without catching anything they would decide to pack up their complicated equipment and go home. And then a small bespectacled clergyman in a deerstalker, with only the most basic rod and line, would suddenly appear. They would stay to watch him. In a matter of minutes he would have landed a fine salmon or sewin, much to the chagrin of the frustrated spectator.

Eric enjoyed a drop of whisky. Fortunately he was married to Doctor Elsbeth, a wise and sensible woman, herself the daughter of another famous Carmarthenshire country parson. She allowed him to enjoy life – but made sure that 'boyo', as she called him, never got too carried away. She often set him tasks to do in the garden while she was at work. As soon as she had disappeared, Eric (so he once told me) would slip across the road to the cottage where Edward Rule the *clochydd* (sexton) lived. He would pass on Elsbeth's orders and Mr Rule would duly come over and do what was needed. Eric would then go out for the day with his brother Mond. He always made sure that they got back before Elsbeth returned. Then he would change swiftly into his gardening clothes and be waiting for her, ready to ask her to admire his supposed handiwork. I very much doubt that Elsbeth was ever fooled by this cunning subterfuge.

Many people (including some of his fellow clergy) dismissed Eric as a 'character'. They couldn't see beyond the deerstalker, the fishing, the politics, the tots of whisky and the endless stream of anecdotes about 'Grey of Brechfa'. A fortunate few were privileged to glimpse something deeper. Clergy are called to be 'fools for Christ's sake' and beneath Eric's apparent folly was a devout and devoted parish priest. Every morning at half past seven Eric would be in St Teilo's Church, tolling the bell before saying *Boreol Weddi* (Welsh Morning Prayer). After my arrival we always said the service together. I had a rectory full of very small children and my sleep was rarely unbroken. Sometimes I wouldn't wake up in time. Eric would start ringing the bell. I'd leap out of bed, throw on whatever garments came to hand, and dash over to the church – knowing that the bell would not stop until I arrived (by which time most of the village would have guessed that their new rector had overslept again).

That was not the only spiritual discipline he passed on to me. He was also very keen on going on a silent retreat once a year and would gather together a small group of fellow clergy to go with him. At times it could be a rather hazardous adventure. I never realised that Eric was blind in one eye until one day, four of us (including a future Bishop of Llandaf), were nearly obliterated by an enormous articulated lorry while Eric was driving us round a roundabout on our way to a monastery in Yorkshire. 'Very sorry – I didn't see that,' he said calmly as the rest of us went into a state of shock.

Eric saw sacramental confession as an important way of keeping a country priest on the straight and narrow. Every Shrove Tuesday he would announce that the time had come for the two of us to be 'shriven' before Lent began. We'd set out across the mountain in his car to find a suitable priest who would listen to our faults and failings and give us absolution and the promise of a new beginning. Shrove Tuesday was also the only day of the year on which Eric smoked (so that he could give up cigarettes for Lent). He always gave up whisky (and alcohol in general) for the penitential season as well, which was more of a sacrifice.

For me, as for others in the parishes, his greatest gift was that of being a pastor and a friend. When I arrived in Brechfa I was dispirited and disillusioned, suffering from the results of overwork, isolation and a certain amount of theological harassment. *'Gwnaiff Eric Grey godi dy galon'* ('Eric Grey will cheer you up') his old friend and neighbour

Archdeacon Sam Jones remarked to me before I moved. He did. And whenever a crisis arose in the parish I would ring him up and receive wise advice and the soothing words 'Paid becso, 'machgen i. Cysga di'n dawel. Mi fydd popeth yn iawn erbyn yfory' ('Don't worry, my boy. Sleep peacefully. Everything will be all right by tomorrow.').

The Celtic tradition places a strong emphasis on the importance of a 'soul friend' as a spiritual guide. Eric's death deprived me of my 'soul friend' and the sense of loss is still there. My idea of Heaven is that it is essentially Brechfa transfigured by the Love of God. If that is so, I am sure that, should I ever end up there, the first person I shall meet will be a short, round, bespectacled priest with a deerstalker on his head and that same old mischievous twinkle in his eye.

Brother Madog's song:
the first Welsh Christmas carol

(Winter 1998)

In a little Welsh country church the children are acting a Nativity play. The building dates back to the thirteenth century. It has a floor of rough stone slabs. A group of small shepherds in home-made bedouin headresses are sitting on some bales near the porch. An angel will soon appear and give them a surprise. In the far corner a local carpenter has built a very convincing stable, with a wooden manger in the centre. Mair and Joseff (Mary and Joseph) begin the journey that will lead them to that stable where Jesus will be born.

The medieval setting recalls the very first Christmas pageant. It took place in 1223 in the little chapel that St Francis of Assisi had built near the village of Greccio. In that simple church Francis recreated the Bethlehem stable. There was a manger filled with straw, and an ox and an ass. People gathered there from the surrounding countryside for a torch-lit midnight mass. Many of them were sure that they could see Francis cradling the Christ-child in his arms. The miracle of Emmanuel – 'God with us' – became intensely real to them.

Francis of Assisi died in 1226. Some ten years later his disciples, the Franciscan friars, reached Wales. Among the stories that they brought with them was the memory of that Christmas night in Greccio. If the wonder of the Incarnation – God become one of us for our sake – could be expressed so vividly in an Italian village there was no reason why that experience should not be shared by communities in Wales. That was certainly the feeling of one of Francis' new Welsh followers: Brother Madog ap Gwallter.

Madog was a poet. That may have been one of the reasons why he felt drawn to join the Franciscans. St Francis had himself been a poet. His glorious *'Cantico delle creature'* ('Song of all created things') had been composed the year before he died. In it he praised the creator God who is revealed in natural things: 'brother son', 'sister moon', 'sister water', 'brother fire', 'sister our mother earth' and even 'sister our bodily death'. Francis' song is often regarded as the first great Italian poem. Ten years after his death another Italian Franciscan poet was born. Iacopone da Todi was to write some of the finest religious verse of the Middle Ages. Brother Madog had become part of a religious order that valued poetry and song as a means of coming close to God.

Madog himself is something of a mystery. Only three of his poems survive, though he presumably wrote many others. The most famous of his works is a meditation on the birth of Jesus. He also composed an ode to God and some verses to Mihangel (St Michael). In the latter he refers to himself as one of Mihangel's parishioners. This suggests that he came from one of the many Welsh Llanfihangels. An extra clue comes from a Cardiff manuscript which contains an anthology of writings selected and gathered by *'Frater Walensis madocus edeirnianensis'* ('the Welsh Brother Madog of Edeirnion'). The link with Edeirnion narrows down the possibilities. Madog was almost certainly a native of Llanfihangel Glyn Myfyr. The great seventeenth-century Welsh scholar Dr John Davies of Mallwyd recorded that Madog's poetry was written around the year 1250. Rhian Andrews, Madog's most recent editor, agrees that his work dates from the second half of the thirteenth century, and notes that both the subjects of his poems and the way in which he handles them are something new in the Welsh poetic tradition.

It is obvious from the way in which he deals with metrical forms that Madog had been trained as a poet in the style of the Gogynfeirdd, the court poets of the Welsh princes. On joining the Franciscans he decided to devote the skills that he had been taught to the service of his new Lord. However as he absorbed the teachings of Scripture and became more and more aware of St Francis' attempt to live out a Christlike everyday existence, Madog became conscious of the need to write a different sort of poetry. Princes liked to be praised in complex, glittering verses. Their egos had to be bedecked with glorious chains of flattering adjectives. The court poets had assumed that God himself should be praised in similar terms. But the Franciscan Brother Madog ap Gwallter, as he knelt beside the Christmas crib, was aware of a God who was not just a distant all-powerful potentate. The creator of everything was also the helpless infant lying in the straw.

Madog prayed and meditated on this startling paradox at the centre of Christianity: the greatest of all becoming the least of all. As he did so a poem began to form in his mind. The words clicked together in familiar patterns of sound. But the ideas shaped by those words were startling. No court poet would ever hint at the possibility of weakness or vulnerability in the ruler whom he praised. The Lord whom Madog served was willing to be shown as a tiny child, clothed in rags. And yet, far from undermining his power and prestige, this willingness to share the depths of human need revealed his true greatness and power.

Brother Madog's song began:

> A Son was given us, a fortunate and privileged Son,
> The Son of glory, a Son to save us, the best of Sons,
> Son of a maiden, whose faith is gentle and whose words are mature,
> Without a human father, this is the gracious Son, giver of blessings.
> We consider wisely and wonder at wonders!
> Nothing more wonderful will ever happen or be spoken of:
> God, the creator of creatures, came to us
> As God, as man, as God-man, with the same gifts,
> A great little giant, a strong powerful weak one, fair of face ,
>
> A wealthy poor one, our Father and our Brother, giver of judgements,
> This is Jesus whom we accept as king of kings,
> Exalted lowly one, Emmanuel, honey of thoughts.
> The world's Lord in the manger of the ox and ass,
> And a heap of hay instead of a cradle for our Lord of hosts;
> He doesn't want embroidered silk or white cloths for his nappies,
> Instead of fair linen there are rags around his bed...

To the audience who first heard those words Madog's message was startling and wonderful. It was natural for the average Welsh man or woman of the thirteenth century to see God in terms of a Welsh prince or a Norman baron or an English king writ large. God, like their earthly rulers, was remote, terrifying, given to destructive whims and the imposing of intolerable burdens. But the Jesus whom Madog ap Gwallter portrayed was different. Here was a 'king of kings' who had every right to live in a castle that would dwarf those of Llywelyn Fawr or English Edward. And yet this God had chosen to share the poverty which was the lot of the ordinary peasant. Listening to the string of paradoxes threaded through Madog's song those impoverished Welsh men and women became aware that there was a God who loved them. Madog himself summed up their surprised elation:

> Christmas Night is a night unlike all evil nights,
> It's a night of joy for the lands of Faith: let us rejoice!

Brother Madog's beautiful meditation on Christ's birth echoes across the centuries. The mysterious paradox of God become man becomes a central theme of Welsh Nativity poems and Christmas carols.

One of the most popular versifiers in Welsh history was Rhys Prichard, the seventeenth-century vicar of Llandovery in Carmarthenshire. Among Prichard's poems in his frequently reprinted *Cannwyll y Cymry* or The Welshman's Candle is *'Awn i Fethle'm'* ('Let's go to Bethlehem'), the opening verses of which are still often sung as a carol:

> Let's go to Bethlehem, all of us singing,
> Jumping, dancing and enjoying ourselves,
> To see our kindly Saviour,
> Born today on Christmas Day.

Vicar Prichard, like Brother Madog before him, becomes entranced by the paradox at the heart of the Christmas story:

> Let's go to Bethlehem to see
> The greatest wonder that's ever happened,
>
> God become a natural man
> So as to die for his people.
>
> Let's go to see the ancient of days,
> Who made the heavens, the sea and the mountain,
> Alpha of ages, Father of light,
> As a little new born child.

> Let's go to Bethlehem to see
> Mary with God's Son on her lap,
> Mary holding between her hands
> The Son who keeps the world from falling.

At the beginning of the nineteenth century similar ideas emerge in the hymns of the young Montgomeryshire farmer's wife Ann Griffiths, Dolwar Fach. Ann, who died before she was thirty, used to recite her verses to Ruth Evans, the maid, while milking the cows and doing other chores around the farm. Ruth was illiterate, but had a tenacious memory. She married John Hughes, a teacher and Methodist preacher. She sang Ann's hymns to him and he wrote them down. They are amongst the finest spiritual treasures in the Welsh language.

Ann was acutely aware of that same paradox that had inspired Madog ap Gwallter. She sang:

> Strange and wonderful with angels,
> A great marvel in the sight of faith,
> To see the giver of being, the great upholder,
> Controller of everything that is,
> In the manger in nappies
> Without a place to lay his head,
> And yet the shining host of glory
> Worship him as the great Lord.

This miracle of the God-man was at the heart of Ann's intense love affair with God in Christ:

> O my soul, see the appropriateness
> Of this divine person;
> Risk your life for him,
> And cast your burden on him.
> He is a man to sympathize
> With all your weaknesses,
> He is God to win the victory
> Over the devil, the flesh and the world.

There is something very fitting about the way in which Ann Griffiths developed her profound insights into the true implications of Christmas while doing the milking in the cowshed at Dolwar Fach. The combination of the deeply spiritual and the earthy and everyday reflect the nature of the Incarnation itself. In the stable at Bethlehem the source of all being becomes a part of the ordinariness of life. The child in the manger is a sign of love. God in Christ has chosen to be like us so that he may understand us and help us to learn to become like him.

Brother Madog's song can still be heard in Wales. The lesson of the 'great little giant' that he learnt from the poor man of Assisi is still being taught by our Nativity plays and Christmas cribs and carols. To some it may seem little more than self-indulgence: a sentimentality that generates a cosy Christmas glow. But others, like Brother Madog and Vicar Prichard and Ann Dolwar Fach before them, look at the figure in the manger and realise that that baby is God – and therefore there will always be hope, even in the darkest times.

A modern Welsh poet who continued to echo Madog's message was Eirian Davies from Nantgaredig in Carmarthenshire, who died earlier this year. In one of his loveliest *englynion* he wrote:

> We know of nothing more wonderful: a Creator
>   Crying in a nappy
> A Baby who could not be weaker,
> God in the world as a Little Child.

If there is a special Welsh voice that can be heard amidst the clamour of a modern commercial Christmas that is it. Words that recall the hidden wonder of the Bethlehem stable. A miracle known only to an old carpenter and his young wife, a handful of excited shepherds, three strange visitors from a far country, and those who still listen out for the gentle music of Brother Madog's song.

Collecting calennigs:
the Welsh New Year – new and old
(Winter 2001)

My younger children are very glad that we are not moving to our new parish in Carmarthen town until February. It means that they'll have a final chance to go around the village collecting calennigs on New Year's morning. They and their friends will go from house to house (avoiding the homes of newcomers to the area who won't know what it's all about) and at each one they'll sing or recite a verse to whoever comes to the door:

> *Blwyddyn newydd dda i chi,*
> *Ac i bawb sydd yn y tŷ;*
> *Dyma ein dymuniad ni:*
> *Blwyddyn newydd dda i chi.*

> ('A good new year to you, and to everyone who is in the house;
> this is our wish: a good new year to you.')

In exchange for the ancient greeting they'll be given a calennig – a New Year's gift. It usually consists of a shiny new coin (often a pound these days) and possibly a tangerine or some sweets as well. By the time that they've finished going round they will have accumulated quite a haul.

An anonymous manuscript history of one of my parishes, written in Welsh almost a hundred years ago, says that at one time the children would start going round to ask for calennigs at midnight and keep on from house to house and farm to farm for the rest of the day. They would carry sacks on their backs to put their presents in. Children in the hills of north Carmarthenshire and elsewhere in Wales have probably been collecting calennigs since before the Romans came.

These days the verses sung by calennig gatherers tend to be rather limited. However in his history of Llandysul, Ceredigion, published in 1896, the Reverend W. J. Davies collected together eighteen different songs sung by children begging for New Year's gifts. Some were cheerful expressions of goodwill – for example:

> *O codwch a goleuwch*
> *Ac hefyd cynnwch dân,*
> *Rhowch barch i'r flwyddyn newydd*
> *Na fu erioed o'r blaen.*
> *Blwyddyn newydd dda,*
> *blwyddyn newydd dda,*
> *blwyddyn newydd dda i chwi,*
> *Hir oes a iechyd,*
> *hir oes a iechyd roddodd Duw i ni.*

('O get up and light the light and also light the fire, show respect to the new year which has never been before. A good new year, a good new year, a good new year to you, long life and health, God gave us long life and health.')

Others contained an element of moral blackmail:

> *Ar ddechreu blwyddyn newydd*
> *A roddwyd gan ein Iôr,*
> *'Rwy'n dod i hôl calennig,*
> *Fel hyn o ddôr i ddôr;*
> *A chofiwch chwithau wrth roddi*
> *I ddiolch am eich ffawd,*
> *Na fuasech wedi'ch geni*
> *Fel finne'n blentyn tlawd.*

('At the beginning of a new year given by our Lord, I come to get a calennig, like this from door to door. Remember as you give to be thankful for your fate, that you were never born as a poor child like me')

The Llandysul children carried sacks and one of their verses tells us what they hoped would be put in them:

> *Mi godes heddyw ma's o'm tŷ,*
> *A'm cwd a'm pastwn gyda mi,*
> *A dyma'm neges ar eich traws,*
> *Sef llanw'm cwd, bara chaws.*

('I left my house this morning with my sack and my walking stick, and here's my message for you: fill my sack with bread and cheese.')

Many children preferred money instead, though sometimes they did not get as much as they might have liked:

> *Mi godes yn foreu,*
> *Mi redes yn ffyrnig,*
> *I dŷ Mr. Jones i 'mofyn Calenig,*
> *Yr oeddwn yn tybied cael swllt neu chwecheiniog*
> *Ond 'nawr rwy'n boddloni ar ddimai neu geiniog.*

('I got up early, I ran furiously to Mr Jones' house to get a calennig. I'd supposed I might have a shilling or sixpence, but now I'm satisfied with a halfpenny or a penny.')

One of the songs had been specially adapted for Llandysul's children by Thomas

Humphreys, a local poet:

> *Dydd Calan yw hi heddyw,*
> *'Rwy'n dyfod ar eich traws,*
> *I fegian am y geiniog*
> *Neu doc o fara chaws;*
> *Mae'n well gen' i gael ceiniog*
> *Gael myn'd i ffair New Inn,*
> *I brynu cacs a fale*
> *Nes byddo mola i'n dynn.*

('Today is New Year's Day, I'm calling on you to beg for a penny or a hunk of bread and cheese; I'd rather have a penny to go to the fair at New Inn, to buy cakes and apples until my tummy's tight.')

Perhaps the most mysterious of the rhymes which Davies collected contains a reference to 'an old English sheep'. Presumably it meant something to those who first sang it:

> *Plant bach sydd yn dyfod*
> *A'u dillad yn dylle,*
> *A'u hewinedd bron codi*
> *Wrth gydio'n y cyde;*
> *O byddwch yn serchog, na fyddwch yn syn,*
> *Mae hen ddafad Seisnig yn byw yn y glyn.*

('Little children are coming with holes in their clothes, and their fingernails almost coming off from clutching the sacks. O be good-natured, don't be surprised, an old English sheep lives in the valley.')

The saddest little verse is one reserved for an absent-minded child who had forgotten all about New Year's Day. He or she would have to tramp from house to house on the second of January hoping that this pathetic plea might touch someone's heart:

> *Calennig yn gyfan*
> *Dranoeth i'r Calan;*
> *Y Calan aeth heibio*
> *Pan nad own yn cofio.*

('A whole calennig the day after New Year's Day; New Year's Day went by and I didn't remember it.')

The word *calennig* comes from *dydd Calan* : New Year's Day. Perhaps it's not surprising that so many New Year songs survived in Llandysul. The small Ceredigion market town is, after all, one of the two places in Wales where the *Hen Galan* or *Calan Hen*

('Old New Year's Day') is still celebrated. In September 1752 Britain changed from the Julian Calendar to the Gregorian Calendar. Wednesday September 2nd was followed by Thursday September 14th. It resulted in riots in some places among those who suspected that the authorities had somehow managed to deprive them of twelve days of their lives.

The people of Llandysul continued to keep the Old New Year. Early on January 12th they would hold a special breakfast for everyone who had helped with the harvest during the preceding autumn. Beer and spirits were consumed in enormous quantities. The feast was followed by a football match, which kicked off at 9 a.m. and continued for the rest of the day. All the revellers took part, using the church doors of Llandysul and Henllan (further along the Teifi valley) as their goalposts. It was a rumbustious affair. Fights would frequently break out and a great many limbs were broken.

By 1833 the Reverend Enoch Jones, Vicar of Llandysul, had got fed up with the violence of the annual football match. He decided to replace it with a festival in which the Sunday Schools from all the surrounding parishes would come together to answer questions about passages from the Bible and sing religious anthems. Perhaps not surprisingly there was quite a lot of opposition from the footballers to this innovation. On one occasion they interrupted the service by kicking the ball in through one door of the church and out through the other, creating havoc as they did so. However it was Enoch Jones' festival which won in the end. The football match withered away, but at the beginning of the twenty-first century the church Sunday Schools of the area still come together in Llandysul on January 12th to celebrate the Old New Year.

On the face of it a Sunday School festival may seem a rather poor substitute for a communal football match. However on the one occasion when I was asked to be among the clergy taking part in Llandysul's *Calan Hen* I was very much struck by the enthusiasm of those taking part. Each church has its own group of participants (many of whom are adults). They recite their allotted *pwnc* (a passage from the Welsh Bible) together. Then they are questioned about it by one of the visiting clergy. Some of the interrogators build up a reputation for being *cas* (nasty) by asking tricky or difficult questions. Others are more soft-hearted (but tend to disappoint many of the onlookers by being so). Each group ends its session by singing a hymn or an anthem. As might be expected there is quite a strong element of competition between the churches that take part in this thoroughly Welsh event.

The other area of West Wales that continues to celebrate the Old New Year is the Gwaun Valley near Fishguard in North Pembrokeshire. The celebrations there have never been reformed by the local clergy. They have however dwindled somewhat in recent years, so I'm told. Apparently the publicity given the event by the media began to draw in a lot of outsiders and the traditional atmosphere of what had been a very local custom was destroyed. However in 1989 the Dyfed Cultural Services Department published a delightful little book entitled *Gwawr yn y Gwaun* (Dawn in the Gwaun). It contained the reminiscences of Pegi Williams, who had been brought up in the valley. The book includes a wonderful description of the way in which *Hen Galan* was celebrated during her childhood.

It was a major festival. The farmers of North Pembrokeshire are famed for the powerful home brew which they produce for special occasions, and the beer for Hen Galan would be particularly potent. There would also be home made ginger beer for the children. A large plum pudding would be prepared as well. The house would be scrubbed from top to bottom in preparation for the expected visitors. Holly would be collected and tied into a 'kissing bush', about the same size as a football, decorated with ribbons and tinsel. This would then be hung between the kitchen and the parlour.

When the Old New Year's Day dawned the men would go off shooting while the women changed into their best clothes and remained in the house to greet the children who came singing for calennigs. They would each be given a coin, a little cake and some ginger beer. Then there would be dinner of roast beef (with potatoes, swedes, parsnips and peas which had been got ready the night before) and plum pudding. The men returned by teatime and saw to the animals and did any other necessary farm chores. Then they changed into their best clothes and went out to meet up with their friends. Until late into the night they would walk from farm to farm. At each house they would stop for a drink of home brewed beer and would sing songs, tell stories, have a bite to eat and generally enjoy themselves.

Pegi Williams' picture of Hen Galan in the Gwaun Valley in the 1920s is a delightful one. The Old New Year provided an occasion for relaxation and celebration for people whose lives were otherwise taken up with a fairly unremitting round of hard physical labour. In their different ways the women, the men and the children were given an opportunity to enjoy themselves. They were aware of the 'new' New Year on January 1st of course, but that didn't stop them from reserving January 12th as their own special day.

Some of my children, along with their friends from the village, will be out collecting calennigs this New Year's Day. Twelve days later the churchpeople of the Llandysul area will come together for *Calan Hen* and some of the folk of the Gwaun Valley will be quaffing pints of strong beer in honour of *Hen Galan*. Anglo-American culture may increasingly pervade all our lives, but at the start of this millennium Wales still has unexpected corners where signs of our uniqueness persist. Hopefully that will remain true for many centuries to come.

The miracle of Dolwar Fach:
Ann Griffiths and her 'world of wonders'

(November/December 2005)

Two hundred years ago a farmer's wife was buried in the churchyard of the remote Montgomeryshire parish of Llanfihangel-yng-Ngwynfa. She was 29 years old. A month earlier she had given birth to a baby girl. The child had only lived for a fortnight. Anyone who has spent time wandering through graveyards and looking at old tombstones, or browsing through early parish registers, will know that the loss of the young mother and her little daughter was a tragedy that was not unfamiliar at the beginning of the nineteenth century. That did not make it less heartbreaking for the bereft widower, who would himself die within three years. What gave this particular event a wider significance, however, was the identity of the wife whose loss was to break his heart. Her name was Ann Griffiths, and she is now widely recognised as one of the most remarkable poets and spiritual writers that Wales has ever produced.

Ann has exercised, and still exercises, a powerful influence on the creative imagination. She has been the subject of two notable literary works that were awarded prizes at National Eisteddfodau. *Fy Hen Lyfr Cownt* by Rhiannon Davies Jones, a novel in the form of an imagined diary, won the Prose Medal in Cardiff in 1960. *Byd o Amser*, a play by Eigra Lewis Roberts, took the drama prize in Carmarthen in 1974. Ann Griffiths was also the subject of a poem by R.S. Thomas, while the Archbishop of Canterbury, Dr Rowan Williams, has translated some of her hymns into English.

Part of the fascination with Ann Griffiths (Ann Thomas before her marriage to Thomas Griffiths in 1804) is the comparatively small amount of material connected with her that has survived. *Rhyfeddaf Fyth…*, the edition of her writings painstakingly edited by E. Wyn James and published by Gwasg Gregynog in an outstandingly beautiful limited edition in 1998, contains all of Ann's hymns. There are thirty of them, several of which consist of a single verse. In addition Wyn James includes the eight letters which she wrote that are still extant.

Biographical sources are equally scarce. Her friend John Hughes wrote the first brief account of Ann's life some forty years after her death. Twenty years later Morris Davies gathered together a few stories and memories of her from the handful of her acquaintances and contemporaries who were still alive. The astonishing quality of her writing has inspired other writers to try to fill in the gaps in her biography. Some of their rather fanciful efforts have gone far beyond anything that the meagre evidence can convincingly sustain.

That Ann Griffiths was a poet is not particularly surprising. Her father also composed poetry and she lived in a community that valued poetic expression. What is more startling is that she expressed her gifts in hymns of quite extraordinary spiritual and emotional intensity and profound theological insight. Ann herself had only had the most basic education. John Hughes, who was himself a schoolmaster, remarked that Ann 'had some schooling in her youth, in order to learn to read English and to write; but she only understood a small amount of English.' When she began to produce her hymns she had so little regard for her own compositions that it is quite miraculous that any of her work has survived at all.

The members of Ann's family were *Eglwyswyr*, devout members of the parish church at Llanfihangel-yng-Ngwynfa, where her father was one of the churchwardens. Even the family's dog went faithfully to church, sitting quietly under his master's seat during the service. From her earliest childhood Ann was familiar with Bishop William Morgan's Welsh Bible and the *Llyfr Gweddi Gyffredin*, the Welsh language version of the Book of Common Prayer, which was used for daily family devotions as well as Sunday services. Her father was also an enthusiastic singer of the lengthy carols, setting out the Christian salvation narrative from Eden to the Second Coming, which formed an important part of the religious and poetic culture of the area, and were particularly linked with the *Plygain* service at Christmas.

Welsh Anglicans like Ann's family saw no inconsistency between their religious devotion and the traditional amusements of their rural community. Her Calvinistic Methodist biographer comments dryly that she was 'fairly wild and frivolous in her youth. She liked a dance…' Morris Davies managed to track down one of her contemporaries who also remembered Ann as an extremely enthusiastic dancer. This may seem a harmless and even a rather admirable trait to a modern reader, but from the standpoint of early nineteenth-century Welsh Calvinistic Methodism dancing was a distinctly shocking and reprehensible activity.

Not that young Ann was especially bothered by criticism from such quarters. John Hughes tells us that she used to mock both Nonconformists and Calvinistic Methodists (the latter at the time were still technically Anglicans, but were rapidly developing into a church within the church). Bala had become the centre of Calvinistic Methodism in North Wales, and people would flock to the special communion and preaching services held there. Ann would make fun of them, remarking "There go the pilgrims on their way to Mecca!"

However, the religious movement that was already having an increasingly profound influence on Welsh life soon began to touch Ann's family. Her elder brother joined the Calvinistic Methodists, having found that the local Anglican priest was unable or unwilling to help him with his spiritual anxieties. When Ann went over to Llanfyllin to join in the dancing at a local festival, a friend persuaded her to go and listen to a Nonconformist minister from Pwllheli, who was preaching in a chapel in the little market town. Something in his words touched Ann deeply and she decided to transform her way of life.

Her initial reaction was to become more faithful in her attendance at the parish church of Llanfihangel-yng-Ngwynfa. However, the priest there seems to have tried to take advantage of her, having invited her back to his house for breakfast after the early morning Christmas *Plygain*. John Hughes says of him that 'his conversations with her in his house were not only irreligious, but too outrageous to be repeated.'

The result was that Ann also felt obliged to look elsewhere for spiritual counsel and support, and she too joined the Calvinistic Methodists.

Early Welsh Methodism placed a strong emphasis both on religious experience and the person of Christ. It was this powerful combination that had helped to inspire the extraordinary body of religious poetry produced by the great hymn-writer of the mid-eighteenth century, William Williams of Pantycelyn. Ann decided to express her deepening spiritual experience in hymns, as William Williams had done. In her case her verses acquired a deeply personal emotional intensity expressed through an exquisite use of Biblical imagery.

In the twentieth century this led to a great deal of speculation about Ann's psychological state at the time when she wrote the hymns. The biographers' references to a carefree girl who enjoyed a dance became embellished so that Ann was recast as a young woman driven by deep sexual obsessions that she could only express through her hymns. Fiction writers homed in on the idea that Ann must have been jilted, probably by a promiscuous ex-dancing partner. The Christ whom she addresses so passionately in her verses would therefore be a substitute for this supposed lost lover.

Such imaginings tend to say more about the culture and attitude that gives rise to them than about the spiritual reality that Ann attempts to convey through her hymns. John Hughes gives a fascinating insight into the way in which her verses were composed, as well as the reason why they did not disappear into oblivion. He remarks that 'Ann once intended to write a diary, as a reminder of the visitations and experiences that she would have; but instead of fulfilling this intention, she began to compose verses of hymns; and whenever something particular was on her mind, it would come out as a verse of a hymn.'

Ann only put a very few of these verses down on paper. Instead she used to recite them to Ruth, her maidservant, to see if she could fit them to a tune. Ruth was unable to write, but fortunately had a very retentive memory. She became engaged to John Hughes, a village schoolmaster who later became a Methodist preacher, and sang Ann's hymns to him. He was so impressed that he wrote them down and thus they were preserved. Morris Davies quotes a conversation between Ann and Ruth, in which the latter said "Mistress, you'd better write those hymns down, as your health is deteriorating. It would be a great pity to lose them." To which the hymn-writer replied calmly, "No: I don't think they are worthy; I only make them for my own comfort."

At the heart of Ann's hymnody is her relationship with Christ. It is significant that the first verse that she is said to have composed is one that describes the nature of Jesus who is both God and man:

> O! f'enaid, gwêl addasrwydd
>   Y Person dwyfol hwn,
> Mentra arno'th fywyd
>   A bwrw arno'th bwn;
> Mae'n ddyn i gydymdeimlo
>   Â'th holl wendidau i gyd,
> Mae'n Dduw i gario'r orsedd
>   Ar ddiafol, cnawd, a byd.

(O my soul, see the fittingness of this divine Person. Risk your life on him and cast your burden on him. He is a man to sympathise with all your weaknesses. He is God to win the victory over the devil, the flesh and the world.)

Like all great mystics Ann had a profound sense of her own personal inadequacy, which intensified her love for the Christ who lovingly accepted her just as she was. In the completed hymn the verse which follows the one that I have just quoted expresses this in an extraordinarily poignant way:

> *Rhyw hiraeth sy am ymadael*
> *Bob dydd â'r gwaedlyd faes,*
> *Nid â'r arch, nac Israel,*
> *Ond hunanymchwydd cas;*
> *Cael dod at fwrdd y Brenin,*
> *A'm gwadd i eiste'n uwch,*
> *A minnau, wan ac eiddil,*
> *Am garu yn y llwch.*

(Every day I have a longing to leave the bloody battlefield – not the ark, nor Israel, but vile self-centred conceit. To be able to come to the King's table, who asks me to sit higher up, while I, weak and helpless, want to love in the dust.)

Another verse, containing a vision of eternal life within the Holy Trinity, was said to have been composed in a mystical trance as Ann was crossing the Berwyn mountains on her way home from a Methodist Communion service in Bala:

> *O! ddedwydd awr tragwyddol orffwys*
> *Oddi wrth fy llafur yn fy rhan,*
> *Ynghanol môr o ryfeddodau*
> *Heb weled terfyn byth, na glan;*
> *Mynediad helaeth byth i para*
> *I fewn trigfannau Tri yn Un;*
> *Dŵr i'w nofio heb fynd trwyddo,*
> *Dyn yn Dduw, a Duw yn ddyn.*

(O happy hour of eternal rest for me from my labours, in the midst of a sea of wonders without ever seeing an end or a shore; a generous everlasting entrance that to the places where the Three in One lives; water to swim in without going through it, man as God, and God as man.)

Perhaps the most quietly impressive picture of the atmosphere in which Ann composed many of her finest verses, however, is the description that an old woman from the area gave to Morris Davies. She remembered the family at their home of Dolwar Fach, spinning and singing carols and hymns, while Ann's father carded the wool. At other times there would be an intense silence. Ann would have an open Bible near her as she span, so that she could pick a verse to meditate on from time to time. "I saw her at her spinning wheel in deep contemplation," the woman remarked, "noticing hardly anything around her, with tears flowing down her cheeks..." Ann Griffiths remains one of God's gifts to Wales: a glorious enigma whose poetry will continue to inspire generations to come.

The finest Welsh language edition of Ann Griffiths' poems and lettes is **Rhyfeddaf Fyth ...**, *edited by E. Wyn James (Gwasg Gregynog). Non-Welsh speakers can get a very real sense of the power of her work from the excellent translations made by Alan Gaunt in* **Ann Griffiths – Hymns and Letters** *(Stainer & Bell). For this article I have made much use of* **Cofiant Mrs Ann Griffiths** *by John Hughes (Aberystwyth, 1854) and* **Cofiant Ann Griffiths** *by Morris Davies (Dinbych, 1865).*

Dewi Sant:
patron saint and national hero
(March/April 2003)

National heroes and patron saints have a special symbolic function. Their characters and actions are frequently re-invented or recast to meet new political or religious needs. That is certainly true of Dewi Sant (St David). For example, Rhigyfarch's Latin Life of St David was composed towards the end of the eleventh century as part of a rearguard action by West Welsh clerics, who were desperate to prevent their diocese being brought under the authority of the Archbishop of Canterbury. The work may give us a few hints about the historical St David, but it tells us far more about the hopes and fears and ideals and aspirations of a native Christian community threatened by Norman aggression.

St David would also be turned into an instrument of church propaganda during the sixteenth century. After the accession of Elizabeth I the scholarly Richard Davies was appointed as Bishop of St David's. He was a renaissance figure and a friend of the English poet Edmund Spenser, who includes a character based on Davies in one his works. Richard Davies was a man of decidedly Protestant views, who had been forced to flee to the Continent for safety during the reign of Queen Mary. Having returned to Wales he was faced with the taunt that he and his fellow Anglicans were 'new men' preaching a new-fangled and alien version of Christianity.

Davies' answer was contained in the letter that he wrote as a preface to the first Welsh translation of the New Testament in 1567. In it he portrayed St David and his contemporaries as representatives of an ancient British church which could trace its origins to the very beginnings of Christianity. He wrote that 'the Britons kept their religion pure and spotless as they had received it from Joseph of Arimathea and from the Church of Rome when she was pure and kept to the rule of God's word.' Davies contrasted this with the debased version of Christianity, which he claimed that St Augustine of Canterbury had brought to the Saxons. His argument was that, far from introducing new and Anglicising changes into the Welsh Church, the Reformers were merely restoring it to its original state. This was an argument which apologists for the Anglican Church in Wales would repeat over the centuries.

Prose writers like Rhigyfarch and Richard Davies are not the only authors to have produced interpretations of St David to suit the needs of their particular place and time. Welsh poets have also turned their attention to our patron saint. Perhaps the most substantial and important example of a praise poem to Dewi Sant was composed by Gwynfardd Brycheiniog, a twelfth-century bard who was the court poet of the Lord Rhys of Deheubarth, the last native ruler of South Wales.

Gwynfardd's great patron had no need to be ashamed of being under the protection of the saint described by his poet. We are told that Dewi is 'of faultless lineage' as the son of 'wise and excellent Sant' (adjectives that seem wholly unsuitable for the royal rapist described in Rhigyfarch's life of St David). The poet's Dewi is a supernatural version of the Lord Rhys, with a somewhat greater sphere of influence than that of the earthly ruler:

> As he wishes, privileged [Dewi] has status,
> And his land is free and glorious;
> Through grace he plays a part in Ireland,
> And Deheubarth and Pebidiog are his;
> And he puts them under the authority of the royal One.

Authority thus flows from God through Dewi to the prince who is under his patronage. But St David makes demands on those who truly wish to follow him:

> Whoever loves Dewi, the good defender,
> Whoever would be his, may he love him like a loved one.
> Whoever loves Dewi, may he never be a deceiver,
> May he never love anger or a rapacious thief;
> Whoever loves self-denying Dewi,
> May he love the mass with numerous clerics;
> Whoever loves Dewi, the good neighbour,
> May he love helping and caring for the needy,
> Whoever loves Dewi as a hard working, wise man,
> Shall be called excellent and powerful.

Gwynfardd portrays the patron saint as a pattern of what a true Christian should be. Those who love him are urged to become like him.

The poet is well acquainted with the territory linked to St David. He lists the many churches that have the saint as their patron. Gwynfardd has visited Llanddewi Brefi and describes the services there with great enthusiasm. He has also been to Mynyw (Menevia – the present St David's) 'at the extremity of Dyfed'. In his description of his hero's power to protect that particular sanctuary Gwynfardd's vivid imagination outpaces the cold facts of history:

> If a heavily armed, threatening fleet comes,
> To terrorise by looting
> Between Mynyw and the sea, terrible things
> Will happen to their host by daylight,
> They shall lose their sight and their lives;
> They will not see the sea or their ships,
> And they'll make an agreement through messengers
> To send gifts swiftly to [Dewi].

A swift glance at *Brut y Tywysogyon* ('The Chronicles of the Princes') reveals a somewhat different and more painful reality: 'Christ was eight hundred and ten years old when the moon went black on Christmas Day. And Mynyw was burnt.' It was also destroyed, ravaged or pillaged in 907, 982, 988, 992, 999 (when Bishop Morgeneu was martyred), 1012, 1022, 1073 (when Bishop Bleiddud was martyred), 1080 (when Bishop Abraham was martyred) and 1091. Political changes meant that it was rather more secure in Gwynfardd's day, but even so his description of the supposed protective powers of the patron saint represents a considerable exercise in wishful thinking.

One fascinating feature of Gwynfardd's poem is the way in which he connects St David with the Welsh language. He describes Dewi's 'good and bold Welsh' and goes on to call him 'learned in Welsh'. The poet also remarks that 'the land of Greece and the territories of Ireland, that Irish-speaking land, quake before Dewi's relics'. There may be an echo here of past conflicts between Welsh and Irish speaking communities in West Wales (or indeed of Welsh speaking subjects struggling to throw off the yoke of Irish speaking dynasties). A part of Dewi's special status had become his guardianship not only of the land and the people within it, but also of the language that they spoke.

Gwynfardd's Dewi is a religious superhero, whose miraculous powers are recounted in stories scattered through the poem. The poet portrays him as a figure on whom the Welsh can rely for help with both their temporal and eternal salvation. At the end of Gwynfardd's song of praise there is a supernatural re-enactment of the Synod of Llanddewi Brefi. That was the occasion when, according to Rhigyfarch, St David was able to create harmony among the argumentative leaders of the Welsh Church (with a little help from the Holy Spirit), uprooting the Pelagian heresy and confirming orthodox teaching.

In Gwynfardd's poem a Synod of Saints gathers together at Llanddewi Brefi. They come from Anjou and Brittany and from various parts of England, from every corner of Wales and from the Isle of Man, Ireland and the Western Isles. Indeed they come from everywhere: 'saints of the world, hosts of the nations'. The purpose of the gathering is to agree to accept 'good-living Dewi' as the greatest saint of all. There is nothing modest or self-effacing about Gwynfardd's enthusiastic Welshness. The implication is that if Dewi is the most important saint of all, the people under his protection are the most special people of all. They are also, through his patronage, the people most likely to be allowed into heaven. Nineteenth- and twentieth-century Welsh people have sometimes been accused of suffering from a 'serf complex' which turned them into doormats that their more powerful and self-assertive neighbours would wipe their feet on. Gwynfardd Brycheiniog certainly never suffered from such a crippling sense of inferiority.

Neither did a more modern poet who also created a picture of St David that was intended to serve the spiritual and political needs of Wales in his time. David Gwenallt Jones (1899-1968) returned to the Christian faith after many years as a Marxist atheist. He was attracted by the sacramental and incarnational emphasis of Anglo-Catholicism, and joined the Church in Wales for a time. He left it in protest and returned to the Calvinistic Methodism of his childhood, when a non-Welsh-speaking Englishman was appointed Archbishop of Wales,.

Gwenallt is one of the great religious poets of the twentieth century. His collection *Eples,* published in 1951 contains a remarkable poem about Dewi Sant. The poet, priest and critic Gwynn ap Gwilym once remarked to me that it tells us far more about Gwenallt than it does about Dewi himself. That, of course, is true. For Gwenallt, as for Gwynfardd, Rhigyfarch and Richard Davies, St David has a symbolic significance that transcends the limitations of historical realities. Gwenallt, like his predecessors, creates a Dewi who will speak to what the writer feels are the spiritual and political needs of Wales at his particular time. The result is a work of imagination rather than of historical reconstruction.

He begins by describing the Communion of Saints in which the temporal and the eternal intersect:

> There is no border between two worlds in the Church;
> The Church militant on the ground and the
> Victorious Church in Heaven is the same.
> And the saints will be in the two-one Church.
> They come to worship with us, a little congregation,
> The saints, our oldest ancestors,
> Who built Wales on the foundation of
> The Crib, the Cross and the Empty Grave;
> And they go out as before to wander through their old familiar places
> And to bring the Gospel to Wales.

Gwenallt's Dewi wanders through the land from county to county 'like God's gypsy with the Gospel and the Altar in his caravan'. He visits universities and schools 'to teach us the purpose of learning.' He goes down the mines and into the steelworks 'to lead the industrial proletariat into his disreputable Church.'

He also brings Christ into the intimacy of domestic life:

> He brought the Church to our homes,
> Putting the Sacred Vessels on the kitchen table,
> Getting bread from the pantry and bad wine from the cellar,
> And standing behind the table like a tramp
> In case he should hide the wonder of the Sacrifice from us.

For Gwenallt, Dewi's Gospel sets the concrete realities of human life in the context of the sacred:

> After Communion we had a chat by the fireside,
> And he talked to us of God's natural Order,
> The person, the family, the nation and the society of nations,
> And the Cross keeping us from turning any of them into a god.

St David is portrayed as the guardian of a Christian nation, whose task is to make Wales aware of its special place in the divine order:

He said that God formed our nation
For His own purpose,
And that her death would damage that Order.

And then the saint erupts with anger at his people for 'licking the backside of the English Leviathan' and allowing themselves to be turned into 'Pavlov's dogs'. The poet's reaction to this outburst is to ask for Dewi's 'forgiveness, strength and sharpness.'

Gwenallt ends the poem with a request to the departing visitor to 'give the Lord Jesus our poor congratulations' and ask if we can join him in heaven at the end of our lives. That final plea echoes the endings of religious poems by medieval bards like Gwynfardd Brycheiniog. A part of the traditional function of a patron saint is to help his or her people find a safe lodging for eternity.

Dewi Sant has been a powerful symbol through the centuries. He is a figure whom writers have used to examine and express the intertwining of Welsh identity and political and spiritual aspirations. Recasting St David for our new millennium is a major challenge for contemporary Welsh poets and artists. There is a sense in which he has come to represent the soul of our nation. If that soul is lost the future will be very uncertain indeed.

William Morgan:
scholar, bishop and hero

(January/February 2005)

In 1988 there were celebrations all over Wales to mark the four hundredth anniversary of the first translation of the complete Bible into Welsh. I was rector of the Carmarthenshire hill parish of Brechfa at the time, so I wrote a bilingual play about the translator, Bishop William Morgan. The children and young people of the church performed it on the Sunday before St David's Day. The climax of the drama came when William Morgan was sitting in his study, working away at his masterpiece. Suddenly a group of the smallest children, representing the villagers of his parish of Llanrhaeadr-ym-Mochnant, erupted onto the scene, chanting: "William Morgan is no good! Chop him up for fire wood!" They then acted out a rather convincing riot with enormous enthusiasm. The translator calmly continued writing.

The following morning the younger members of the cast of the play were back in the village primary school. Mrs Davies, the infant teacher, asked her charges, *"Nawrte, blant. Beth ydych chi'n gwybod am William Morgan?"* ("Now then, children. What do you know about William Morgan?"). The reply was immediate, loud, unanimous and stated with firm conviction: "William Morgan is no good! Chop him up for fire wood!" Which showed that the play had left its mark on its young performers, even if it had not had quite the effect that I had intended. At least the children must have been aware that William Morgan translated the Bible at a time when he was faced with a great deal of hostility.

That the translator should ever have been in a position to undertake such an enormous task is a sign of his remarkable intellectual and spiritual qualities. William Morgan was born in Tŷ Mawr Wybrnant (Tyddyn Mawr) in the parish of Penmachno in 1545, the son of a tenant farmer on the Gwydir estate. A puzzle that has challenged his biographers is how someone from such a remote and isolated household could have come to have a firm grounding in the classical languages. It has often been suggested that one of the monks expelled from the nearby abbey of Maenen at the dissolution of the monasteries may have found shelter in Tŷ Mawr and have paid for his keep by providing the boy with tuition in Latin and possibly Greek as well.

Although this theory makes an attractive story, there is no concrete evidence to support it. What is certain is that the young boy was bright enough to attract the attention of his father's landlord. There is evidence that Morys Wyn, squire of Gwydir between 1558 and 1580, provided free education for suitable sons of his tenants. The squire employed an Anglican clergyman as his personal chaplain. One of the chaplain's duties was to teach these children. Among William Morgan's fellow pupils was almost certainly the poet Edmwnd Prys, who would later become Archdeacon of Meirionnydd and author of the Welsh metrical psalms.

The squire of Gwydir's brother had been a fellow of St John's College, Cambridge, and therefore it is hardly surprising that their patron sent William Morgan and Edmwnd Prys there for the next stage of their education. William arrived in Cambridge in 1565. He became a 'sizar', which meant that he was able to pay his way through university by acting as a servant to students from wealthier backgrounds. Despite these additional duties, he found time not only to develop into a brilliant scholar, but also to make friends with a group of extremely gifted Welshmen who were also studying at Cambridge. These included Richard Vaughan from Llŷn, who would become successively Bishop of Bangor, Chester and London, Gabriel Goodman from Denbighshire, the future Dean of Westminster, William Hughes, later to be Bishop of St Asaph, and Hugh Billot, another future Bishop of Bangor and Chester. His old acquaintance Edmwnd Prys was also a member of the circle.

Cambridge was a centre of Protestant thought, and this outstanding group of Welsh-speaking church leaders would play a crucially important role in winning the ordinary people of North Wales over to Anglicanism. William Morgan apparently spent thirteen years at the university, by the end of which time he had become a master of the Hebrew language as well as Latin, Greek, French, German and his native Welsh. He was ordained in Ely Cathedral in 1568 and appointed as vicar of Llanbadarn Fawr in 1572 and Welshpool in 1575. However it is unlikely that he ever actually served in either of these parishes. The appointments were apparently intended to provide him with an income to enable him to continue to pursue his studies.

Then in 1578 Morgan came back to Wales and was inducted to the parish of Llanrhaeadr-ym-Mochnant in southern Denbighshire. He left the academic debates of Cambridge behind him, remaining in this rural community until 1595. It is probable that he had already embarked on the project of translating a complete Welsh Bible before his arrival in Llanrhaeadr. The New Testament had been available in Welsh since 1567 in the version prepared by William Salesbury, assisted by Bishop Richard Davies and Thomas Huet. It was a translation that was desperately in need of revision. Salesbury had a great many idiosyncratic theories about Welsh grammar and spelling and these had severely limited the user-friendliness of his work. It was said that a particularly extreme example of the scholarly layman's pedantry sparked a quarrel with Richard Davies, which led to the two of them abandoning their project to translate the Old Testament as well.

The lack of a Welsh Old Testament caused a specific problem for parish clergy in much of Wales. They would read the service and the New Testament lesson in Welsh, but the Old Testament lesson was in English. Since very few, if any, among the members of the average Welsh congregation understood English, they quite naturally concluded that that part of the service was in Latin, and it became known as '*Yr Offeren*' ('The Mass'), much to the annoyance of ardent Protestant reformers. This confusion must certainly have brought home to William Morgan the need for a Welsh Bible that was clear, comprehensible and complete.

Llanrhaeadr-ym-Mochnant seemed, on the face of it, a peaceful community that would be an ideal setting for a scholarly clergyman to finish a major piece of work. Unfortunately the reality proved rather different. Shortly after arriving in the parish the new vicar decided to get married. He chose as his wife a widow named Catrin. Unfortunately this upset some local gentry who had designs on the widow's inheritance. They were even more annoyed when William Morgan helped a son from the Gwydir family, his old patrons, to marry a wealthy local heiress, whose hand and lands had been earmarked for one of their own offspring.

The quarrel led to accusations and counter-accusations, and soon William Morgan found himself before the Court of the High Commission in London, where Dr John Whitgift was appointed to examine the Welsh clergyman. Whitgift had been Morgan's theology professor at Cambridge. He was now Bishop of Worcester and would soon move on to become Archbishop of Canterbury. The prelate gave short shrift to the trumped up charges against his former pupil. William Morgan then told Whitgift about the translation that he had been working on, and confessed that the project was in jeopardy because he had no money left. The English bishop's response was both generous and enthusiastic. He promised to give the Welsh scholar all the financial help that would be needed to ensure the success of the project.

That may have removed one burden from William Morgan's mind, but his parochial anxieties continued. The family that had taken against him continued to make all sorts of dark and dangerous threats. They stirred up a mob from among his parishioners, who proceeded to riot outside the vicarage, throwing stones through the windows (the scene that the children of my village church re-enacted with such enjoyment). They also arranged for people to withhold their tithes, thus depriving the hard-pressed vicar of a considerable portion of his income. At one point things became so fraught that Morgan had to keep a loaded pistol under his priest's cassock for self-protection. He even took it to church with him.

And yet, despite these constant conflicts and pressures, the work of translating the Bible continued. It may be that his scholarly activities provided William Morgan with a blessed escape from the storms that raged around him. By 1587 his Bible was complete. It included both the Old and New Testaments and the Apocrypha. The next task was to see this massive volume through the press. This presented an additional hurdle. There were no printers in Wales at this time and the work had to be done in London. Accuracy was especially important. A small misprint could have disastrous consequences. In 1632 there would be the notorious case of the English 'Wicked Bible', so-called because the word 'not' was inadvertently left out from the seventh commandment, with the result that it read 'Thou shalt commit adultery'. The slipshod printers were arrested and savagely punished.

Because the London printers knew no Welsh, Morgan had to travel to London to oversee the printing of the Bible in person. Archbishop Whitgift not only remembered his promise and paid for the production of the volume, he also offered free lodgings for the Welshman at Lambeth Palace. Morgan politely declined. It was more convenient to stay which his old friend Gabriel Goodman, the Welsh-speaking Dean of Westminster Abbey, who lived on the same side of the Thames as the printers. By September 1588 the lengthy process of proof reading and printing was at an end. The people of Wales had a complete translation of the Bible in their own tongue for the very first time.

The poets received the volume ecstatically, pouring out verses in praise of its translator. It was fitting that they should do so, because Morgan had drawn on the Welsh poetic tradition in crafting a form of Welsh prose that would be accepted in all the different dialect areas of Wales. The four basic dialects of Welsh at the time were roughly coterminous with the boundaries of the four ancient Welsh dioceses: Bangor, St Asaph, St David's and Llandaff. To achieve such linguistic unity was in itself little short of a miracle. Moreover Biblical scholars have also praised William Morgan's translation for its accuracy. Although most of his work had been done in the comparatively remote community of Llanrhaeadr-ym-Mochnant, far away from universities and major libraries, he had managed to make use of some of the best original texts then available.

In 1595 William Morgan was duly rewarded by being promoted from the troublesome parish of Llanrhaeadr to become Bishop of Llandaff. There he set to work on another necessary project. The *Llyfr Gweddi Gyffredin* (Welsh Book of Common Prayer) was still essentially the volume produced in the 1560s by William Salesbury and Richard Davies, and its stylistic oddities continued to trip up the clergy who used it. William Morgan set about producing a Prayer Book that would have the same clarity as his Bible. This appeared in 1599 and would shape the devotional life of the majority of Welsh-speaking Christians for many years to come.

After five years in Llandaff the bishop was moved back to his old diocese of St Asaph. There he embarked on a revision of his Bible. Time and circumstances meant that he never completed it. The revised version would eventually be produced in 1620 by Bishop Parry of St Asaph and Dr John Davies of Mallwyd. William Morgan died at his home in St Asaph on 10 September 1604. He was a poor man. His financial contribution towards the project of translating the Bible, and the cost of defending the law suits into which he had been drawn by his enemies, meant that he had many debts. His total possessions were valued at £110/1/11 (roughly £110 10p), while the worth of everything in the room in which he died was a mere £3/18/3 (roughly £3 91p). The spiritual and literary value of the Bible that he left to the people of Wales was, however, beyond all price.

Battle of the bishops –
The fight for Welshness in the Church in Wales
(Autumn 2002)

Chapels have been an important feature of Welsh life during the past couple of centuries. It may therefore be something of a surprise to discover that at the beginning of the eighteenth century the overwhelming majority of Welsh people belonged to the Anglican Church (the Church of England in Wales, as it was then). One of the key factors that turned Wales from a 'church' to a 'chapel' country was the appointment of a succession of non-Welsh-speaking bishops to Welsh dioceses. These prelates became known as the *'Esgyb Eingl'* ('Anglo Bishops') and their collective impact on the life of the Welsh Church was disastrous in the extreme.

In the period between the accession of Queen Elizabeth and the death of Queen Anne there had been some very distinguished Welsh Anglican Bishops. The earliest example was Bishop Richard Davies of St David's, a former Protestant exile who features as a character in one of Edmund Spenser's poems. He turned his palace at Abergwili into a centre of Welsh renaissance learning, encouraging and assisting William Salesbury in his translation of the New Testament and the Prayer book into Welsh.

In 1588 a complete Welsh Bible was produced by Dr William Morgan, who was consecrated Bishop of Llandaff in 1595, moving to the marginally wealthier see of St Asaph in 1601. His successor there, Bishop Richard Parry, was responsible for the revised version of the Welsh Bible in 1620. The impression given by these men is one of scholarly prelates dedicated to the spiritual needs of their dioceses. Even the cantankerous Carmarthen-born Bishop Lewes Bayly of Bangor (who was briefly imprisoned by James I for an outspoken remark about foreign policy) was the author of *The Practice of Piety*, a devotional handbook that was one of the seventeenth century's best selling volumes.

In the latter half of the seventeenth century some outstanding Welsh-speaking bishops were still being appointed. William Thomas, Bishop of St David's between 1677 and 1683, encouraged and assisted the nonconformist preacher Stephen Hughes in his work of publishing the religious verses of Vicar Prichard of Llanymddyfri. The most impressive of all the Welsh bishops of this period was William Lloyd, Bishop of St Asaph from 1680 to 1692. He insisted on conducting all his Confirmation services in Welsh and held open debates with representatives of the Quakers, Independents and Presbyterians. Lloyd was also one of the 'seven bishops' imprisoned in the Tower of London by James II.

Bishops of Lloyd's calibre might have revived, renewed and strengthened the Welsh Church. However John Wynne, who was consecrated Bishop of St Asaph in January 1715 and moved to be Bishop of Bath and Wells in 1727, was to be the last native Welsh bishop until the appointment of Joshua Hughes to the same diocese in 1870. For a century and a half the Welsh Church would be ruled by men who did not speak the only language understood by the vast majority of their flock. Many of these prelates would only infrequently and unwillingly visit their dioceses, preferring to remain either in London or elsewhere in England.

By the early decades of the nineteenth century it had become clear that the future of the Anglican Church in Wales was in the balance. In 1831 the Royal Cambrian Institution in London awarded a prize to Arthur James Johnes, a young man from Montgomeryshire, for his Essay on the Causes of Dissent in Wales. Johnes, who later became a distinguished barrister and judge, was a close associate of a group of cultured Welsh-speaking clergy known as *'yr hen bersoniaid llengar'* ('the old literary parsons'). They were concerned with ensuring the survival of such key elements of Welsh cultural life as eisteddfodau (which were frowned on by the chapels at that time). They also fought tooth and nail for what was left of the Welshness of the Church of England in Wales.

Johnes's essay was a damning indictment of the way in which the church was being run. The key problem was the system of patronage.

The most important diocesan appointments and the wealthiest parishes in Wales were all in the gift either of the 'Anglo Bishops' or of church dignitaries, colleges and other institutions in England. Few of these patrons could resist the temptation to award such generously endowed livings to their relations or friends, who were almost always non-Welsh speaking Englishmen. The native Welsh clergy usually ended up as starveling curates, paid a pittance to do the work for these well-heeled dignitaries.

The essayist focussed on the Diocese of St Asaph. Between 1660 and 1745 the 'higher preferments' (best-paid posts) in the diocese had been held by 43 Englishmen and 60 Welshmen. But between 1745 and 1830 the Welshmen had almost been eliminated altogether: 73 Englishmen had been appointed to these plum positions and only 10 Welshmen. The most notorious nepotist was John Luxmoore, a Devonshire man, who was Bishop of St Asaph between 1815 and 1830. Luxmoore appointed his son as Dean of the Cathedral and Chancellor of the Diocese, and generously shared out many of the richest parishes among his closest relatives.

Not all the 'Anglo Bishops' were as shameless as the appalling Luxmoore. One of them even stands out as a conscientious reformer.

Thomas Burgess, Bishop of St David's, made great efforts to ensure that his clergy were properly trained, establishing St David's College, Llanbedr-pont-steffan (Lampeter), for Anglican ordinands in 1822. Burgess was unique among the 'Anglo Bishops' because of his genuine interest in Welsh culture. He enthusiastically supported the 'old literary parsons' and was admitted to the Gorsedd of Bards by Iolo Morganwg on the first day of the Carmarthen Eisteddfod of 1819. However Burgess moved back over Offa's Dyke to become Bishop of Salisbury in 1825 and his successor in West Wales was a more characteristic 'Anglo Bishop'.

John Banks Jenkinson, the new Bishop of St David's, was the first cousin of Robert Banks Jenkinson, Lord Liverpool. Lord Liverpool also happened to be the Tory Prime Minister at the time (and therefore the person who was responsible for appointing Welsh bishops in those pre-disestablishment days). As with the selection of many other 'Anglo Bishops' political and personal loyalties were conveniently combined. Lord Liverpool was confident that his cousin would use his vote as a bishop in the House of

Lords to support the Tory cause. Jenkinson, a shy and hideously hen-pecked scholar, was also Dean of Durham Cathedral and felt much more at home in the Deanery there than in the Bishop's Palace at Abergwili.

The 'old literary parsons' were not the only Welsh clergy to be appalled by the damage done by the 'Anglo Bishops'. Almondbury is now an attractive suburb of Huddersfield. In the 1820s it was an enormous parish with a population that had expanded rapidly as a result of the industrial revolution. Its vicar was an energetic Welshman from Ceredigion named Lewis Jones, locally known as 'the church-building parson'. He divided his vast parish into fifteen smaller ones and staffed them with gifted clergy from West Wales who had been unable to obtain suitable parishes in their native land. He then formed them into a pressure group, the 'Association of Welsh Clergy of the West Riding of Wales'. From 1835 onwards they began a vigorous campaign to secure Welsh-speaking bishops for Wales.

The matter came to a head in 1840 when Bishop Banks Jenkinson died at Great Malvern. A campaign was immediately started to ensure that the new Bishop of St David's should be a Welsh-speaking Welshman. There was one obvious and outstanding candidate. William Bruce Knight was Chancellor of Llandaff Diocese. He was also a distinguished scholar in both Welsh and Hebrew. He had rescued the Welsh Bible from the hands of the eccentric lexicographer William Owen Pughe, who had wanted to use it to propagate his own bizarre theories about Welsh spelling. Knight was also the leading light in the team that was engaged in revising the Welsh Prayer Book. In addition to his scholarly gifts, the Chancellor of Llandaff was a brilliant administrator and an energetic church builder with a flair for raising the money to pay for his various projects. He was quite obviously the man for the job.

Lord Melbourne, the Prime Minister, was bombarded by pleas from Knight's supporters. The Reverend David James *('Dewi o Ddyfed')*, a former curate of Almondbury who had moved to a parish in Liverpool, brought the pressure of the Liverpool Welsh to bear on Downing Street. All the Welsh Members of Parliament except one backed his campaign for a Welsh-speaking bishop for a Welsh-speaking diocese. The Archdeacon of Brecon wrote to Melbourne recommending Knight. The Welsh newspapers were wholeheartedly in favour of such an appointment. It seemed that at last Wales was going to have another Welsh Bishop of the calibre of Davies, Morgan and Lloyd. Then the Prime Minister announced his decision.

He had chosen another Englishman. Connop Thirlwall was in the middle of writing an eight-volume history of Greece. He had made a name for himself by translating one of the works of the German theologian Friedrich Schleiermacher into English. This led him to be regarded as a dangerous liberal by conservative English churchmen, who voiced their disapproval of his appointment. The Welsh were more troubled by his linguistic deficiencies. What was only too clear was that Thirlwall's appointment had nothing do either with theology or language. The new bishop, like the Prime Minister, was a Whig. Melbourne was only interested in making sure that he replaced Banks Jenkinson the Tory with one of his own supporters.

The sense of outrage in Wales was intense. *Yr Haul* ('The Sun' – not to be confused with its modern English equivalent) was the leading Welsh church magazine, edited by the brilliant satirist David Owen ('Brutus'). He voiced the feelings of his fellow countrymen. 'Would the English accept a Welsh Bishop ministering to them through the Welsh language?' Brutus asked – and answered 'They wouldn't, they would unite to speak out against such injustice. Why must we Welsh accept this? Are we orangutans or some species of monkey? Have we or haven't we got souls? Do religious service and spiritual things truly pertain to our condition or are they just our empty dreams? Are our children to be considered as higher than the chicks of swallows? We now think that we can have nothing to do with religion, or that the way to heaven is so easy that one of the Emperor of China's Mandarins can guide us there by telling us sing, ching, ja-jee, bo-ko-chi!'

Brutus's withering attack was echoed by journalists from every part of Wales. David James, the Liverpool clergyman, wrote an open letter to Connop Thirlwall, listing all the reasons why a non-Welsh-speaking bishop was unsuitable for a Welsh-speaking diocese and trying to persuade him to refuse the appointment. Despite the furore Thirlwall's consecration as Bishop of St David's went ahead.

The new bishop did however decide to make a serious attempt to learn Welsh. In October 1840 he visited the Abergavenni Eisteddfod and was welcomed with a speech (in Welsh) in which he was praised for learning the language so well in such a short time. He responded (in English) by admitting that his knowledge of Welsh was extremely limited, but added that, given the position which he had the honour of filling, he considered that learning the language was a most important and sacred duty.

Connop Thirlwall spent 34 years as Bishop of St David's and proved a devoted and conscientious bishop. He became fluent enough to preach in Welsh and after his death some of his Welsh sermons were collected and published. It is a volume that requires a good deal of stamina. The original owner of my copy read nine of the twelve sermons before giving up – and I have yet to reach halfway. There is something strangely sleep-inducing about Thirlwall's Welsh. Still, at least he made the effort, which is more than can be said for his many predecessors among the 'Anglo Bishops'. Thirlwall's successor was a Welsh-speaking Welshman from Ceredigion. By then the 'Battle of the Bishops' had been won.

Patrick's pilgrimage:
walking to St David's

(Winter 2003)

The Venerable Archard Williams was one of those dynamic Welsh Victorians who managed to combine a startling variety of activities. As well being Archdeacon of Carmarthen he was editor of the *Carmarthen Journal*, headmaster of the Grammar School, director of the gasworks, chaplain of the prison and the asylum, a county magistrate, vice-chairman of the Board of Guardians, rural dean and perpetual curate of one country parish and rector of another. However the position that brought him most satisfaction was that of being the first incumbent of the parish of Carmarthen St David.

Archard Williams' father had been a curate of the historic parish church of St Peter's, Carmarthen. This was very Anglicised, and the elder Williams argued strongly for the need for a second church in the town to serve Welsh-speaking Eglwyswyr. Before he had an opportunity to carry this project through, Williams senior died. Archard, who was only four years old, was left as an orphan. Fulfilling his father's dream became the son's ambition. The foundation stone of Eglwys Dewi Sant (St David's Church) was laid in 1835. The church was opened two years later and consecrated in 1841.

The new church was in a prominent position at the west end of the town, making it visible from far around. Archard made sure that the tower of Eglwys Dewi Sant looked down on that of St Peter's, the English church on the other side of Carmarthen. One unusual feature of the new building was that it faced from north to south. In 1843 St David's was made a separate district of St Peter's Parish and fourteen years later it became an independent parish.

In the year that St David's achieved district status Carmarthen became the focus of one of the most important protest movements in modern Welsh history. The major roads in west Wales were run by turnpike trusts, which set up tollgates to charge travellers. In a time of agricultural depression the burden of tolls became intolerable. Farmers who went to collect lime to fertilise their fields would discover that the value of their load was less than the money that they had paid at the tollgates. In 1839 the tollgate at Efailwen was smashed by *'Merched Beca'* ('The Daughters of Rebecca') and before long gates were being broken down throughout west Wales. The Rebeccaites did their work at night, blackening their faces and wearing women's clothes as a disguise. They took their name from the blessing given to Isaac's wife in the book of Genesis, which includes the words, 'let thy seed possess the gates of those which hate them'. On June 19th 1843 Rebecca's Daughters marched on Carmarthen.

At that time Carmarthen was a major Welsh port, with something of a reputation for riotous behaviour. The Rebeccaites intended to present a petition of grievances to the local Mayor. They broke down the Water Street tollgate and marched into the town behind a large banner proclaiming *'Cyfiawnder a Charwyr Cyfiawnder ydym ni oll'* ('Justice and we are all Lovers of Justice'). They never reached the Mayor. The Carmarthen mob hijacked the procession and led it off to the much-hated town workhouse, which was ransacked enthusiastically. Then, unexpectedly, the cavalry arrived. The 4th Light Dragoons quickly rounded up a hundred prisoners, while the other more fortunate rioters made their escape as best they could.

One result of the Rebecca Riots was that a garrison of soldiers was permanently stationed in the west of Carmarthen. They were marched over to Eglwys Dewi Sant on Sundays, which meant that English-language services were introduced. The church became crowded and Archard Williams decided both to expand it and turn it round to a more conventional east-west axis. His plans were grandiose in the extreme, and there have been suggestions that he wanted to persuade Bishop Connop Thirlwall (who lived at Abergwili, just outside Carmarthen), to abandon St David's Cathedral and use St David's Carmarthen as a much more accessible pro-cathedral. That never happened, and Archard's new building, although very beautiful, was on a smaller scale than he had originally intended. The overcrowding eased when, in the late 1860s, the English-speaking congregation left to found Christ Church, down the road. The moving spirits behind this included an ex-army officer who had come from England to Carmarthen to put down the Rebecca riots, and doubtless suspected that the Welsh-speaking congregation was a nest of secret Rebbecaites.

Victorian vanity can create problems for later generations. Archard's Eglwys Dewi Sant, although superficially attractive, was rather badly built. Its structural flaws only came to light on November 5th 2003 when the gable end of the nave of the church collapsed through the roof of the chancel causing enormous damage. Fortunately no one was hurt. My curate, Jane, and I had been saying Morning Prayer a few hours before. Some of the falling masonry landed on our seats and we would certainly have been killed if the collapse had happened while we were sitting there. To cheer her up, I reminded Jane that, in the Middle Ages, to be crushed by a falling church wall was seen as a sign of divine judgement, whereas for a wall to cave in just after you had left the building was regarded as definite proof of sanctity.

Welsh church insurance covers damage from falling masonry, but not Victorian jerry-building. Our small but faithful Welsh-speaking congregation suddenly had to raise £85,000 to put the fallen wall back. In a fit of rash enthusiasm (prompted perhaps by my close escape) I volunteered to undertake a fifty-mile sponsored pilgrimage on foot from St David's Church, Carmarthen, to St David's Cathedral in Pembrokeshire. The members of the church responded to the suggestion with enthusiasm. A pilgrimage committee was set up immediately. In Welsh-speaking Wales committees are so much a part of our way of life that we even a verb pwyllgora ('to committee'). Fortunately the members of this committee were hugely efficient and arranged the route with great care and precision.

The pilgrimage began on a bright Tuesday morning in February, with a cheerful send off by the Mayor of Carmarthen and the Chairman of Carmarthenshire County Council. We plodded westward along the A40 for a few miles and then branched off to the little village of Bancyfelin. We were now in the territory of the Mayor of St Clears, who joined us while we passed through his domain. Both he and I have been engaged in teaching Welsh to adults, and as we trudged along we discussed the finer points of that underrated calling.

I stopped for a few minutes by Llanfihangel Abercywyn Church to do a live broadcast about the pilgrimage for Radio Cymru, the Welsh-language radio station. Llanfihangel is the resting-place of Canon Conrad Evans, one of the gentlest and kindest priests I have ever known. He was vicar of Abercywyn for many years and was well known as an actor on Welsh-language radio and television. After his retirement he worshipped faithfully in Eglwys Dewi Sant.

It was from Canon Conrad's book, *The Story of a Parish*, that I learnt that the Blue Boar in St Clears, where we stopped for lunch, had its own connection with the Rebecca Riots. The St Clears area was a hotbed of Rebeccaism. In December 1842, at the request of the local gentry, the Home Office sent Inspector George Martin and two police constables from London to try to restore order. They made their headquarters at the Blue Boar, and it was from there that the Inspector sent his gloomy reports to the Carmarthenshire magistrates. His chief complaint was that, although he enrolled a large number of labourers and journeymen as special constables, most of them were sympathetic to the rioters. When he tried to recruit local farmers he was even less successful. Many of them actually were 'Daughters of Rebecca'.

From St Clears we walked on to Whitland *(Hendy-gwyn ar Daf)*. Once again a friendly Mayor greeted us. He escorted us to Canolfan Hywel Dda, where a feast had been prepared for us. Hywel Dda was a powerful tenth-century Welsh ruler who is credited with holding an assembly at Whitland at which the Welsh laws were codified. It has been suggested that some of the representatives who attended the meeting may have going to St David's as pilgrims, so it was appropriate that we should call in at the hall and gardens that form the attractive modern memorial to Good King Hywel.

Our second day began with a blessing from the Vicar of Whitland, after which we set off on the back road through Lampeter Velfrey to Narberth. Narberth *(Arberth)* has had a mysterious resonance in my mind ever since I studied Pwyll Pendefig Dyfed as an undergraduate. I recalled the story of Pwyll sitting on the mound at Arberth and waiting to see a wonder. It turned out to be Rhiannon, the horsewoman, riding by at a steady pace that was still too fast for any of Pwyll's followers to overtake her. We were welcomed to Narberth by the Lady Mayor. She presented me with a scroll allowing me safe conduct through the attractive little town.

The afternoon slog proved the most difficult of the journey. We walked for several miles along a dreary stretch of the A40, on a grass verge churned up by moles and field mice. Medieval pilgrims were spared the endless stream of traffic that rushed past us with a constant deafening roar. I was very grateful for the staff, carved with the head of Dewi Sant, which one of my parishioners had kindly given me to help me on the pilgrimage. It was a great relief when Haverfordwest Golf Club, the end of our second leg, appeared on the horizon.

Canon Derek Evans blessed us at the start of the third day. We then made our way down the hill into the medieval market town of Haverfordwest, where the Mayor whisked us into his parlour for an official reception. There are a many hills between Pembrokeshire's county town and St David's and my feet had acquired several blisters along the way. However any thoughts that our expedition might have been even remotely heroic were put firmly in perspective when we stopped for lunch at a delightful restaurant called the Keeston Kitchen. It turned out that our generous and welcoming hosts had also once undertaken a sponsored walk – but their effort had been across the Himalayas.

Between the steep hill at Newgale and the village of Solfach, our afternoon destination, is the ancient parish of St Elvis. It has always puzzled me that one of the greatest American singers of the twentieth century should share a name with the patron saint of an obscure Pembrokeshire parish. Elvis is the English equivalent of Aelfyw, who is said to have baptised Dewi Sant. According to Irish tradition, Aelfyw was illegitimate. After his birth he was left outside on a rock to die. A she-wolf took pity on the infant and suckled him. Later on, having become a bishop, Aelfyw is said to have rescued his foster-mother from a party of hunters

Our final morning was a glorious walk along the Pembrokeshire Coastal Park to St Non's, the traditional birthplace of St David. We stopped there for a picnic and then made our way down to the Cathedral, where the Dean, the Very Reverend J. Wyn Evans, welcomed us and celebrated the Eucharist for us at the High Altar near the Shrine of St David. "There have been many pilgrims to St David's over the centuries," he remarked, "from now on they will be divided into two categories: pre-Patrick and post-Patrick." He also suggested that I should have come to the Cathedral on the traditional route that led past *'Dŵr Cleifion'*, the place where medieval pilgrims bathed their weary feet. My feet were indeed extremely painful, but the pilgrimage had raised £12,000 towards the cost of restoring Eglwys Dewi Sant, so I couldn't really complain.

Healing waters and a hunted hare:
two Celtic women saints from Wales

(Autumn 1998)

The sixth-century 'Age of Saints' left Wales with many places of pilgrimage. St David's became a major religious centre, drawing lay and clerical visitors from throughout the Celtic lands. Poets and princes expressed their wish to be buried on Bardsey Island *(Ynys Enlli)*, among the graves of thousands of saints. Those looking for healing made their way to one or other of the sacred springs that could be found near almost every early Welsh church. Flowing water was as much a source and symbol of life to the Christian Celts as it had been to their pagan forebears.

Perhaps the most famous of the healing springs was at Holywell *(Treffynnon* – 'the town of the spring' – in Welsh). Its origins were linked to one of the most famous and popular legends of the Welsh Middle Ages. This told the story of a devout young woman called Gwenfrewi (Winifred in English), the daughter of a powerful chieftain from Tegeingl, the modern Flintshire. Gwenfrewi decided that God was calling her to become a female hermit. Her father invited his brother-in-law, the great and ferocious St Beuno, to come to the area to give her the necessary spiritual preparation and training.

Beuno was delighted. His original monastery had been at Berriew in Montgomeryshire. He had abandoned it after hearing a huntsman using a strange language (English) on the far bank of the Severn. After a short stay with the saintly Tysilio at Meifod, Beuno had tried to settle at Gwyddelwern near Corwen. There he quarrelled with the grandsons of the local ruler and had to move on once again. The offer of some land to build a cell and chapel in exchange for the training his niece in the religious life was too good to refuse. Beuno settled at Sychnant.

But one Sunday, while Gwenfrewi's parents were at Mass, a young nobleman named Caradog called at their house. He had been out hunting. It was a hot day, and he asked for a drink to quench his thirst. Gwenfrewi brought it to him. Caradog took a violent fancy to her, and began to force his attentions on the girl. She wriggled out of his clutches and went into an inner room, saying that he should wait for her while she changed into her Sunday dress. Then she slipped out of the back door and ran off towards Beuno's chapel, hoping that her uncle would be able to protect her.

Caradog soon realised that he had been tricked. Leaping on his horse, he set off after Gwenfrewi. He caught up with her by the door of the little chapel. He was furious with rage at being spurned. Drawing his sword he cut off Gwenfrewi's head with a savage blow. The head rolled along the ground, and where it came to rest the rock opened up and water gushed forth. This spring would become St Winifred's Well, one of the holy places of north Wales.

The commotion attracted Beuno's attention. He rushed to the door of the little church and saw the headless body of his niece and the young nobleman holding a sword dripping with blood. Unfortunately for Caradog, his victim's uncle was renowned for his virulent curses. Beuno zapped Gwenfrewi's murderer with a particularly powerful imprecation. Caradog immediately dissolved away like wax melting in front of the fire. It is said that his luckless descendants always found themselves barking like dogs whenever they ventured near Holywell. This was seen as a long-lasting side effect of Beuno's curse.

Fortunately for Gwenfrewi, her uncle's other speciality was putting the heads back on decapitated people and restoring them to life. He did this so successfully in Gwenfrewi's case that only a little white scar remained on her neck as a reminder of her ordeal. She was so grateful for her uncle's kindness that she promised to weave him a monk's habit every year and send it to him as a sign of her thanks. The restless Beuno soon moved on from Sychnant, eventually founding the greatest of his churches at Clynnog Fawr in Arfon, where he died and was buried.

Gwenfrewi lived for another fifteen years, becoming the superior of a community of female hermits at Gwytherin in Denbighshire. In 1138 her bones were removed to the Abbey at Shrewsbury. The monks there renamed her Winifred and spread the story of her miraculous resuscitation far and wide. Soon pilgrims were making their way from every corner of Britain to venerate the relics of this famous holy Welshwoman, filling the abbey's coffers with tokens of their respect. Devotees of Shrewsbury Abbey's most famous (if imaginary) Welsh monk – Ellis Peters' Brother Cadfael – will know something about this tradition.

The other woman from the 'Age of Saints' who has left her mark on Welsh storytelling is linked to a tradition that is far less lurid and laced with improbabilities than that of Gwenfrewi. Tucked away in a remote and very lovely Montgomeryshire valley is a tiny church. At one time it was intended to take the roof off and allow it to become a ruin. Instead in recent years a dedicated priest carefully restored the ancient sanctuary and shrine of the person after whom the church is named. Melangell (Monicella in Latin) was the daughter of an Irish king. Her story survives in a sixteenth-century manuscript. It is one of the loveliest of all the legends of the saints of Wales.

It begins, like the Mabinogion, with a hunting scene. Brochwel Ysgythrog ('Brochwel of the tusks') was ruler of a greater Powys that in the sixth century included most of what is now Shropshire. He had left his court at Pengwern (Shrewsbury) and ventured into one of the farthest corners of his territory, taking his dogs with him. The hounds started a hare and chased after it until it disappeared into a thorny thicket. Brochwel came up to investigate and was startled to find a beautiful woman hidden away among the thorns and brambles, deep in prayer.

The hare had taken refuge under the hem of this stranger's cloak. It stared out calmly at the dogs, as if daring them to try to attack it. The prince yelled at his hounds, urging them to catch the hare. But instead of rushing forward the dogs retreated, howling mournfully. The carving on the fifteenth-century rood screen in the church shows Brochwel on horseback, the hounds, the hare and the woman. It also shows Brochwel's huntsman blowing his horn to encourage the two very anxious looking dogs. There is a tradition (either portrayed by the screen or resulting from imaginative storytelling based on the carving) that the huntsman's horn stuck to his lips when he tried to sound it.

Prince Brochwel was understandably rather taken aback by all this. He asked the woman how long she had been living in solitude in such a wild part of his lands. She answered that she had been there for fifteen years, and that this was the first occasion in all that time that she had seen a man's face. The tusky ruler then enquired about her origins (that standard Welsh set of questions: *"O ble 'dych chi'n dod? Ydych chi'n perthyn i fel-a-fel?"* "Where are you from? Are you related to so-and-so?"). The stranger told him that her name was Melangell and that she was the daughter of an Irish king. She had wanted to dedicate her life to God, but her father had different plans for her. He had arranged to marry her off to an influential Irish nobleman. To avoid this fate Melangell had fled across the sea to Wales, trusting that God would lead her to a place of safety. He had guided her to Pennant, the isolated valley that had become her home.

The prince was impressed by Melangell's story. The way in which her presence had protected the hare from his hunting dogs had also left its mark on him. He decided to grant Pennant to Melangell, making it a place of 'perpetual asylum, refuge and protection'. In the often brutal centuries that were to follow in Powys the existence of this inviolable sanctuary provided a ray of hope for men and women who were fleeing for their lives. As long as they didn't use Pennant Melangell as a base for any illegal activity they would be safe from their pursuers there.

Melangell's protection didn't just extend to the unfortunate wretches who sought refuge in her valley. The author of her legend tells us that she lived on for another thirty seven years after Brochwel's visit. During that time the wild hares befriended her and would come and visit her every day as if they were her pets. They became regarded as her special creatures that were not to be harmed in any way. In the seventeenth century the local name for them was 'Melangell's lambs'. If people from the district came across a stranger hunting a hare with dogs, they would shout out "God and Saint Melangell be with you!" – and it was said that the hare would then invariably escape.

Other women came to join Melangell in her life of quiet prayer. Gradually a community of female hermits was established in her peaceful valley, similar to the one of which Gwenfrewi was abbess at Gwytherin. Shortly after Melangell's death the tranquil life of this group of holy women was savagely interrupted. A man named Elise decided that the nuns of Pennant were a tempting target. He arrived at Pennant Melangell, intending to kidnap and rape the women. Not only was he unsuccessful, he apparently came to a sudden and very unpleasant end. The brief reference to the event in the old manuscript gives no further details. One can only assume that Melangell's sisters were more than capable of looking after themselves.

Melangell's memory has left its mark on the landscape of her valley. Craig Melangell ('Melangell's rock') is an outcrop where she is said to have gone to pray. Gwely Melangell ('Melangell's bed') is a cleft in the rocky hillside where Melangell was believed to have slept. More important, however, was the fact that her body was buried within the church. In the twelfth century Melangell's remains were apparently removed from her grave and put in a beautifully constructed shrine, made by local craftsmen. This became the focus of her cult, and was visited by medieval pilgrims. The shrine was decorated with carvings representing luxuriant foliage. One recent commentator has suggested that this might have been a reminder of the thorny, brambly thicket where

Brochwel Ysgythrog first came across Melangell.

Sometime after the Reformation the shrine was destroyed. Substantial parts of it were, however, preserved. They were carefully built into the lych-gate and the fabric of the church. This may be an indication of the continuing affection of the people of the valley for their saint and her story. It has meant that it has been possible to reconstruct the shrine, which now stands in the chancel of the little church. In recent years the story of Melangell and the hare has begun to draw a substantial number of modern pilgrims from Wales and beyond to visit her burial place and to become aware of the inner peace and stillness that can be found there. The Reverend Evelyn Davies, the woman priest in charge of the little church, has a ministry of prayer, counselling and healing which in many ways echoes that of Melangell herself.

The stories of Gwenfrewi and Melangell have been too well told for far too long for it to be possible to sift out the facts from the fiction. But at their heart is a memory of courageous Christian witness. Both women had decided to respond to a particular spiritual calling. Both were prepared to face extremes of danger and difficulty in order to do so. That there memory has been cherished and revered over the centuries in Wales is an indication of the special qualities of their lives. In a society that was often brutal and chaotic they gave a glimpse of other, better possibilities.

A lost innocence:
Welsh May carols in peace and wartime

(March/April 2005)

'*Clame*' (Calanmai or May Day) was a time of joy and celebration in early seventeenth-century Wales. The dozing inhabitants of scattered farmhouses and cottages would be wakened from their slumbers by a visit from one of the local musicians. Two May carols have survived that were composed around the year 1625 by Siôn ab Ifan. He was a *crythor* – a player of the *crwth*, a venerable Welsh musical instrument whose popularity was fatally undermined by a combination of Calvinistic Methodist disapproval and the introduction of the violin.

Siôn began one of his carols with suitably flattering references to the members of the family whose sleep he had interrupted. He thanked God for the fertility of the land and the animals, expressing his gratitude for the early arrival of spring. Then he called the young men and women of the household to take part in the rituals associated with the day: customs that had their origins in the fertility rites of pre-Christian times.

The young men were told to go out to the woods to gather and bring back birch branches. These they would present to their girlfriends, who would themselves have been busy in the meantime. Their traditional task was to gather herbs and flowers from the gardens, so that they could decorate their windows to welcome their lovers. There was no sense of prurience or disapproval in the poet's instructions. The May celebrations represented God-given Nature taking its course. Siôn ended the song by asking a divine blessing on the household and its barns and fields and orchards, and in his other carol he remarks that Jesus himself is glad to see May Day.

This second carol suggests that not everyone was delighted to be woken up before dawn by the *crythor* even at '*Clame*'. It includes an apologetic verse in which the musician remarks that he hopes that his audience will not be angry at being roused from their beds. Another stanza was probably reserved for those households where the response was particularly hostile:

> I'll wander along now – I didn't get much of a welcome here.
> May my Lord God keep you contented where you are.
> Christ's blessing on your hearth and on your bed.
> Get up when you want to.

'*Clame*' apparently induced a generosity of spirit in Siôn ab Ifan that enabled him to withstand even the frostiest reception. He ended this carol, dated 1625, with a request for God's blessing on the new king, Charles I, and his advisers. Then, with a swift farewell and thanks for the coins that had been thrown at him, he set off for the next house.

There is a delightful innocence about Siôn ab Ifan's May carols. It is hardly surprising that one of his favourite adjectives is '*paradwysedd*' ('paradise-like'), because the world that he describes is very much like Eden without the snake. The rhythms of that world are natural ones, the gifts of a generous Creator God. May-time is verdant, fruitful and full of life. Even when there is a hint of imperfection, the *crythor* sets it right by introducing Jesus as a kind of supernatural vet, who comes to help the weaker animals in their need. Unfortunately Siôn's earthly king was soon to be embroiled in a conflict that would destroy that sense of paradise.

In September 1644 the war between King Charles and Parliament penetrated into the heart of mid-Wales. Early in the month Sir Thomas Myddelton, a Parliamentarian commander, succeeded in capturing a large supply of gunpowder from the small Royalist garrison at Newtown in Montgomeryshire. He then took over Montgomery castle, storing the captured gunpowder there. The Royalists retaliated by besieging the castle. Three thousand Parliamentary troops then marched towards it to attempt to raise the siege. New recruits also flooded in from across North Wales and the border counties to strengthen the Royalist army.

A major clash was inevitable. It took place on the nineteenth of that month. The supporters of Charles I suffered a crushing defeat. Five hundred of their men were killed, and the remaining one thousand five hundred captured. The Welsh regarded the Stuarts as the heirs of their own Tudor dynasty and overwhelmingly backed the king. One Cavalier officer described Wales as 'the nursery of the king's infantry.' It is therefore not surprising that the casualty lists after the battle of Montgomery contained a large number of Welsh names. Only forty Parliamentarians lost their lives, and less than sixty were wounded. Archbishop John Williams, one of the Royalist leaders in North Wales, regarded the rout at Montgomery as even more disastrous than the defeat at Marston Moor earlier in the year.

One of those who was almost certainly both a witness of the battle and involved in burying the victims of the carnage was Wmffre Dafydd ab Ifan, the *clochydd* (sexton) of Llanbrynmair. His calling meant that he was very experienced at digging graves. Like many of his fellow *clochyddion*, he was also a poet, and one manuscript credits him with having introduced carols for the first time into the pre-dawn Christmas *Plygain* services of North Wales.

In 1645, several months after the battle of Montgomery, Wmffre composed a May carol. It began conventionally enough, calling on the people of the parish to get up on a fine and quiet May morning to go out and listen to the cuckoo's song:

> The leaves of the trees are turning green,
> Verdant by your houses.
> There are beautiful green shoots,
> There are mountain pastures full of fruit,
> And this at the start of gracious, gentle May.

But the mood of the carol started to change with the introduction of a disturbingly apocalyptic chorus:

> Get up, men, get up
> To repent,

> To try to deserve peace
> From the Man who is above.
> Fortune's wheel has turned to the furthest point;
> As is praiseworthy, concern yourself with God,
> In case the world is coming to an end.

The old innocence of May had gone. God continued to be generous, but in return humans were proud and hard-hearted. In a sad time of rebellion there was only room for repentance. The *clochydd* called on Welshmen and Englishmen to go down on their bare knees and pray to God for forgiveness and peace.

And then the source of the desperation that colours Wmffre's carol emerged. He began to describe the horrors that he had witnessed. Suddenly we are a world away from the playful pastoral paradise of Siôn ab Ifan the *crythor*. The gravedigger from Llanbrynmair's verses seem closer to the work of the First World War poets. He sang of a drum beating the alarm, of excessive bravado and confused attacks, and of music made by fire and gunpowder and the whizzing of leaden bullets, rather than by the strings of *crwth* and harp.

Plundering, rifling, raping and the ransacking of houses followed. Blood cried out for vengeance:

> The bodies of our neighbours,
> And our brothers and companions
> Are great mounds of blue carcasses
> In the clay.
> Their bones are in heaps.
> They are buried in ditches –
> And this in the pure and lovely season of May…
>
> Ravens and birds without number
> Are feeding
> On the flesh and blood of our brothers,
> And the Lord is punishing us
> For our abominable wrong…

And still the trumpet continued to sound, the cannon continued to roar and bodies were ripped to pieces with merciless cruelty.

The *clochydd* also told of other side effects of the Civil War. Taxes were oppressively high, horses were requisitioned for use by the army, news was scarce and people no longer dared to travel far. Castles, towns and great houses had been burnt and scholarship had been abandoned. Yet even at this low ebb in the monarch's fortunes, Wmffre still saw Charles I as the only one who could restore the familiar order and rhythm of life. He asked God to save and defend the king and all his supporters and to wipe out his enemies. The gravedigger's prayers were not answered. The Royalists were defeated.

The Interregnum period saw the introduction of strict rules and penalties aimed at restricting traditional courting customs and eliminating pre-marital sex. It seems unlikely that these measures were particularly successful, but they certainly angered the Cavalier poet Huw Morys, a flirtatious young bachelor. He penned some bitter verses attacking the '*Ystatud dieithr ynfyd*' ('strange stupid Statute') that threatened both his girlfriend and himself with imprisonment.

Even after the Restoration of Charles II, Welsh May carols never quite recaptured their old atmosphere of carefree innocence. One that was composed by Huw Morys, probably around 1664, certainly began promisingly enough:

> Devout joyful family,
> Wake up and listen to my muse,
> As you look at the earth's beautiful surface
> With its green leaves.
> Good signs show
> That a lovely summer is near.
> The bare trees now
> Wear green breeches
> To welcome May Day
> And the days of good blessings.

Morys described God as the source of the miracle of growth, one result of which was that there would be 'milk for the women and children, and beer for the men and their foster sons.' Only the proud and the miserly would be denied God's blessing. But even in the midst of all this plenty there were rumours of approaching war that upset the general cheerfulness. The poet advised his listeners to ignore such stories, telling them that the best way to be happy was to stay at home singing the praises of May, instead of going off to France or Holland.

Unfortunately such a blithe head-in-the-sand approach became increasingly difficult to sustain. The Great Plague of 1665 and the Great Fire of London the following year helped to foster apocalyptic gloom. When Richard Rowland wrote a May carol in 1667 he began traditionally with descriptions of leafy trees, blooming flowers, honey-making bees and singing birds. But then the May birch tree reminded him of the parable of the fig tree in St Matthew's Gospel, in which Jesus had made hints about signs that the end of the world was nigh.

Having started to think in this way, the poet soon spotted all sorts of disturbing omens. The songs of the cuckoo, the thrush and the blackbird made him think of Christ's trumpet calling the dead to the Last Judgement. Even the young girls who played such an important part in the traditional May rituals prompted Rowland to recall the story of the wise virgins waiting to meet the bridegroom with their lamps – a parable about preparedness for the Second Coming of Christ.

Rowland's fixation with the end of the world was not shared by later May carol writers, but the sense of lost innocence persisted. Siôn Dafydd Las, composing a May carol in the aftermath of William of Orange's defeat of the Roman Catholic James II, couldn't resist a dig at 'cruel base unworthy graceless Romish traitors.' The May carols composed by Huw Morys in the closing years of the seventeenth century had a more traditional feel, but even in his verses it was clear that the untrammelled freedom of the years before the Civil War had not been recovered.

Cromwell's regulations had infuriated Huw during his younger days. Now there were new restrictions. The restored Church of England in Wales wanted to reduce the number of illegitimate births. It used diocesan courts to police sexual behaviour. As a devout Anglican Huw was theoretically in favour of this, but as the author of some of the most beautiful Welsh love lyrics his true feelings were rather different. In one May carol he advises lovers carried away by leaves and flowers to 'remember the court of Llanelwy (St Asaph).' In another the warning is even starker:

> Lads who are greatly in love,
> Think about treading carefully,
> Without trying a wanton tumble
> In order to catch a girl.
> The bishops' law
> Is to fine the rich
> And to punish the bodies of the poor
> Until the fountain of love grows cold.

No doubt he felt genuine *hiraeth* for the carefree paradise-like days of Siôn ab Ifan the *crythor*.

'Vile George' and Twm Penpistyll:
the troubles of a village rebel

(July/August 1999)

At the beginning of the nineteenth century the authorities in West Wales were feeling distinctly nervous. In 1797 a French invasion had been swiftly defeated at Fishguard by the Castlemartin Yeomanry, assisted by the redoubtable red-flannel-skirted, pitchfork-wielding Jemima Nicholas. Nevertheless the possibility of seditious activity and rebellious behaviour remained a worry. There were some suspicious characters hidden away in the Carmarthenshire hills. The most suspect of all was a certain Thomas Evans, a weaver, preacher and poet from the little village of Brechfa.

To his neighbours, Thomas Evans was 'Twm Penpistyll', after the farmhouse where he and his family had made their home. It's the name by which he is still known in the area where he once lived. In literary circles Twm became 'Tomos Glyn Cothi', the inheritor of the mantle of Carmarthenshire's great fifteenth-century poet Lewys Glyn Cothi. It was as Tomos Glyn Cothi that Twm had taken part in the first Welsh assembly of the Gorsedd of Bards, held at Bryn Owain (Stalling Down) in Glamorgan in 1795.

Twm had become a close friend of Iolo Morganwg, the founder of the Gorsedd. The two were on the same literary, spiritual and political wavelength – though Twm seems to have avoided the opium habit which fired some of Iolo's wilder imaginings. They shared an interest in collecting, copying and studying Welsh poetic manuscripts. Both were Unitarians. Twm had been expelled from the Independent chapel in Gwernogle because of his heretical beliefs. His response had been to found a chapel of his own, tucked away on the slope leading down from his home to Cwm Cothi. A sharp-sighted rambler can still glimpse the ruins among the trees. The Brechfa weaver had produced several Unitarian pamphlets in Welsh and corresponded with some of the leaders of English Unitarianism. His religious opponents nicknamed him 'Priestley bach' after his hero, the brilliant scientist and Unitarian thinker Dr Joseph Priestley. Twm was not offended by this. He even called one of his sons Joseph Priestley Evans.

Unitarianism and radical politics went together. Priestley had become notorious through his publicly expressed support for the principles of the French Revolution. In 1791, on the second anniversary of the fall of the Bastille, Priestley's house, laboratory and library in Birmingham were destroyed by an angry mob. Twm shared Priestley's political views. He translated the Marseillaise into Welsh, and the first of the three issues of the *Drysorfa Gymmysgedig* or *Miscellaneous Repository*, a short-lived magazine which Twm edited between 1795 and 1796, contained a song which called on the 'Almighty Father' to 'scatter those who grow fat on human blood'. His most savage scorn was reserved for the Prime Minister, William Pitt. In a Welsh verse addressed to this 'butcher' and 'traitor', Twm calls him 'Pitt the oppressor who loads burdens on the backs of the hard-pressed poor'. He punningly refers to this *'Pwll uffern'* (Pit of hell), asking 'Who can like your cold black twistings?'

Then in 1797 the ragtag French army under its drunken American commander landed at Strumble Head near Fishguard. Their defeat by the local Welsh yeomanry filled Twm with a patriotic pride that swept away his pro-French sympathies. He wrote a song about the invasion in which he describes how the 'proud worldly men who had once conquered the Austrians and Prussians at the same time' were forced to beg for mercy 'at the feet of the brave Welsh'. The revolutionary had suddenly become a loyalist. Yet in 1801 Twm was to be arrested for seditious behaviour and imprisoned in Carmarthen jail.

The charge against Twm was that he had loudly, aggressively and very publicly sung a revolutionary verse (in English) praising the French and attacking George III:

> *And when upon the British shore*
> *The thundering guns of France shall roar,*
> *Vile George shall trembling stand*
> *Or fly his native land,*
> *With Terror and Appal,*
> *Dance Carmagnol, Dance Carmagnol.*

This constituted 'seditious, opprobrious and inflammatory words reflecting on his present Majesty's person and government' which might have 'alienated the affections' of any loyal subjects who heard them. In fact the only 'vile George' who was really connected with the affair was not the ageing, increasingly dotty British monarch. It was the ringleader of the three men who accused Twm of this treasonable behaviour: George Thomas, the Brechfa cobbler.

The quarrel between George Thomas and Twm Penpistyll had begun in the little breakaway chapel in Cwm Cothi. At first George had been one of Twm's small band of followers there. Then something had gone terribly wrong. George was accused of 'improper and even very immoral conduct'. It was said that he had 'relapsed into openly professed Atheism'. Such behaviour provided the Unitarians' religious rivals with useful ammunition. The Brechfa Calvinistic Methodists and Anglicans and the Gwernogle Independents already regarded Twm as a dangerous heretic. Now they could accuse him of encouraging not just liberty but libertinism: moral anarchy and atheism of the sort connected with the wildest French radicals. There was only one way in which Twm could defend himself and his congregation. George Thomas was excommunicated and expelled from Cwm Cothi Chapel. This public humiliation must have fuelled the fires of village gossip for some time. Worse was to come.

The *'Cwrw Bach'* (literally 'little beer') was one of the ways in which West Wales communities rallied to help the needy and indigent in the days before the Welfare State. It was basically a party held to raise funds for someone who had fallen on hard times. The person involved would offer whatever valuable item remained in their possession as the prize in a raffle in which all his or her neighbours took part.

The event got its name from the beer that was always brewed in large quantities to lubricate the occasion and add to the general cheerfulness.

In March 1801 it was decided to hold a *'Cwrw Bach'* to help Thomas Jones, who lived in a wretched hovel on the edge of Brechfa village. The poor man offered his watch as the raffle prize and Daniel Jones, landlord of the Forest Arms, promised to ensure that there would be an adequate supply of beer. Tickets for the raffle were sixpence each and a large number of people gathered on the appointed evening to try for the watch and to imbibe the *cwrw*. Both Twm Penpistyll and George Thomas joined their fellow-villagers for this charitable occasion, whose modern equivalent would be a crowded 'tip-it' match in the Forest Arms in aid of the local hospital.

At first things went smoothly. Twm was asked to write down the names of all those who paid their sixpences. The paper with the names on it was then cut up and put into a hat for the draw. George Thomas and one of his cronies were in charge of the draw itself. George's friend's name was on the first bit of paper to be pulled from the hat. He was immediately accused of fixing the raffle. Tempers became frayed and peace was only restored when the raffle was re-drawn. The watch was won by someone else and then the second stage of the '*Cwrw Bach*' began. This was an impromptu Noson Lawen, with people taking it in turns to sing songs.

Some of the songs were sentimental. One was a Welsh translation of Thomas Gray's *Elegy in a Country Churchyard*. More rousing was Twm's 'Welsh Marseillaise. As the evening drew on people began to sing satirical verses, most of them referring to the faults and failings of George Thomas the cobbler. George was furious. He suspected that Twm, as the village poet, was the author of these insults. He decided to get his revenge. While the Unitarian preacher dozed peacefully in Penpistyll, sleeping off the effects of Daniel Jones's *cwrw*, George Thomas was on the road to Carmarthen, his mind filled with the accusations that he was going to make against his enemy.

George's stratagem succeeded. Twm was put on trial, convicted and sentenced to two years in prison and to two public appearances in the pillory in Carmarthen. For a man with a wife and nine children depending on him for their support this was devastating. Fortunately Twm's friends, neighbours and fellow Unitarians energetically set about collecting money to help the destitute family. Twm himself sent a carefully worded appeal for clemency to George III. It was turned down despite the heart-rending reference to the 'unfortunate Petitioner and ... his innocent, unprotected and deeply suffering family'. The judges who had been asked to comment on the case approved the verdict, noting that 'the Prisoner was in the habit of composing, singing and teaching others to sing songs in the Welch language of very seditious tendency.'

The pillory was intended to humiliate. It stood in the square outside the gateway of Carmarthen castle. Passers-by could jeer or throw things at the prisoner who was on display there. The Carmarthen mob (famed for its unruliness) was kind to the Unitarian preacher. This was apparently because Twm carefully stage-managed his pillorying with the help of a kindly (or generously bribed) jailer. The details in different accounts vary slightly, but it seems that two of Twm's pretty young daughters, dressed in their best white frocks, were positioned on either side of the pillory while he stood in it. The little girls won the crowd's sympathy. The only person to throw anything at Twm was a bad-tempered old woman who chucked an egg at him. As it broke in his face she was (so the story goes) immediately overwhelmed with remorse and begged him to forgive her.

The remainder of Twm's sentence passed quietly. He devoted his time in prison to producing a thematic dictionary which was one of the first books written to help English-speakers learn Welsh. It included a useful section of helpful phrases for English travellers calling in at Welsh hostelries. This would enable (for example) a visitor to the Forest Arms in Brechfa to stable his horse and order a pint of gin without the slightest difficulty.

Meanwhile yet another 'vile George' was gunning for him. Lord George Murray was one of the many improbable and inappropriate Englishmen whom successive prime ministers kept appointing as bishops of Welsh dioceses for over a century and a half. He was an expert on signalling by semaphore and an enthusiastic recruiter of soldiers and militiamen to fight the French. In 1801 he became Bishop of St David's. Lord George discovered, shortly after his arrival at the palace in Abergwili, that there was a genuine Welsh-speaking subversive languishing in Carmarthen jail nearby. This made him very excited indeed.

Colonel Edward Despard, a disgruntled Irish former colonial administrator, had dreamed up an ambitious conspiracy. The army was to mutiny, Londoners were to rebel, George III would be assassinated and the Tower and the Bank of England would be captured. Despard's plot was betrayed. He was arrested in November 1802 and executed the following year. As soon as news of Despard's conspiracy reached the bishop's palace Lord George put pen to paper. He informed the Home Secretary in London about 'one Thomas Evans, an Anabaptist teacher, now in Carmarthen Gaol, under conviction for seditious practices.' The bishop thought him 'a very likely person to have papers in his possession which might lead to some discovery.' The Home Secretary was not convinced. He politely informed the bishop that Twm could not have been involved in the conspiracy. He had, after all, been imprisoned months before Colonel Despard hatched his fantastic plot.

On his release Twm returned to Brechfa and his large family. For nine years he lived a deliberately quiet existence, keeping his head down and hoping that the authorities would forget about him. He compiled a Unitarian hymnbook from hymns that he had written. Presumably he avoided even the most tempting 'Cwrw Bach' and gave up singing political songs. In 1811 he moved to be minister of the Unitarian Meeting House in Aberdare. The Reverend Thomas Evans, 'Tomos Glyn Cothi', respected preacher and literary figure, died in 1833. But in a corner of the Carmarthen hills the story of Twm Penpistyll and 'vile George' lives on.

The tribulations of Trynihid:
the painful legend of Saint Illtud's wife
(Autumn 2000)

Llanilltud Fawr (or Llantwit Major) in the Vale of Glamorgan was one of the great intellectual centres of the early Welsh Church. St Illtud, the founder of the monastic school there, was praised by one of his contemporaries as 'the refined master of almost all Britain'. A Breton monk, writing some time after Illtud's death, remarked that he 'was of all the Britons the most accomplished in all the Scriptures, namely of the Old and New Testaments, and in those of philosophy of every kind, of geometry namely, and of rhetoric, grammar and arithmetic....and by birth he was a most wise magician, having knowledge of the future.'

These descriptions show clearly that the historical St Illtud was a remarkable scholar. He lived in middle of what are sometimes called the 'Dark Ages': the period following the collapse of the Roman Empire. In that troubled time Illtud drew light from three sources. He combined the Christianity which had begun to flourish in late Roman Britain with classical learning and the traditional wisdom usually associated with the druids. This threefold combination underlay the teaching which he passed on to the students who came to his monastic school.

Centuries passed and the memory of the historical Illtud faded. Around the year 1090 Lifris, Archdeacon of Glamorgan, wrote an account of the saint's conversion to the religious life. He depicts Illtud as a soldier in the service of a chieftain named Poul of Penychen. Some of his comrades force St Cadog to give them twenty loaves, a barrel of beer and a fat sow, so that they can have a feast. Illtud, who hadn't been with them on the raid, rides up as they are preparing the feast. Suddenly the ground opens up beneath the greedy warriors and they disappear into a deep abyss. As the only survivor Illtud immediately asks to join Cadog's monastery at Llancarfan.

Illtud the soldier saint – Illtud Farchog ('Illtud the knight') quickly captured the medieval Welsh imagination. Yet in fact the Archdeacon's story was really the product of local church rivalry and the political pressures of the time. Lifris was also Master of St Cadog's foundation at Llancarfan. There could be no better way of asserting its superiority over Llantwit Major, its ancient rival, than by telling a story which made Illtud a convert and pupil of Cadog.

At the time that the account was written the Normans had just swept into South Wales. Their leaders were warrior barons like Robert Fitzhamon, Lord of Glamorgan. Lifris belonged to the old Welsh tribal church which felt very much under threat from its new rulers. By turning Illtud into a soldier who had experienced conversion and become a monk, Lifris was reminding the new rulers that there was a higher calling than that of bearing arms. The story of the earthquake underlined his belief that the church was superior to the secular power. It may also have been intended to deter any greedy Norman soldiers who might have felt tempted to despoil Llancarfan.

Half a century went by. Norman clerics now dominated the church in Glamorgan. At Llantwit Major Illtud's ancient monastery had been replaced by a collegiate church.

One of the clergy of the new foundation decided to write the life of the saint. The author was aware of the latest literary fashion. Geoffrey of Monmouth's highly imaginative *History of the Kings of Britain* had just established King Arthur as the central hero of early Welsh history. In the Llantwit biography Illtud now becomes King Arthur's cousin in a blatant attempt to boost his standing among up-to-the-minute Arthurian romantics. Even more significant is the depiction of the saint as a married man. His loving wife is named Trynihid.

Trynihid is a good, faithful and virtuous woman. Her husband is head of the military retinue of a King of Glamorgan who is now called Poulentus. The author borrows Lifris' story of the raid on Cadog's monastery, the earthquake and Illtud's conversion. However, as one of the clergy of a rival establishment, he gets rid of any idea that Illtud might have become Cadog's disciple at Llancarfan. Instead, having witnessed the annihilation of his comrades, Illtud leaves Poulentus' service, dons clerical dress, and settles down by the river Nadawan.

Trynihid accepts this sudden change in lifestyle uncomplainingly, joining her husband in a rough riverside shelter made out of reeds. But during their first night there Illtud has a dream. In it an angel appears and tells him that from now on he should devote himself to pious study and prayer. This will involve giving up sex. His wife may be beautiful, but the angel informs him that chastity is even better and will lead him to eternal life. Illtud is ordered to reject his wife and told of a suitable spot in the valley of Hodnant where he can settle as a hermit.

The saint wakes up and tells Trynihid that she should go out and check up on the horses immediately. He doesn't give her time either to put any clothes on or to brush her flowing tresses. She has to go out into the sunlight stark naked with her hair all over the place. When she returns Illtud looks at her and decides that he doesn't find her attractive any more. He makes an extremely unpleasant vow to abandon her. The vow encapsulates his loathing and rejection of the woman whom he had once loved.

Poor Trynihid is not yet fully aware of this dramatic change in her husband's attitude towards her. Having seen to the horses, she quite naturally wants to go back to bed. But Illtud tells her that she has become like snake's poison to him and that he never wants to live with her again. He does however hand over her clothes. Once she has dressed Trynihid sits down at Illtud's feet and tells him that she would be quite happy to starve, if only she could stay with him. But even this doesn't undermine the saint's determination. He firmly turns his back on her and goes off to find the spot which the angel had recommended for his hermitage, and which turns out to be a very lovely place indeed.

After being abandoned in this abrupt and cruel way by her husband, Trynihid decides to devote herself to a celibate life of prayer and good works, helping widows and poor nuns. She is described as having a particularly deep personal devotion to the Holy Trinity (this is no doubt something to do with her name). The rejected wife becomes a hermit, following Illtud's example. She builds herself a cell and an oratory at a lonely place in the mountains. And then one day she decides to visit her husband, who by this time has become the abbot of a monastery. It is not a wise move.

As she approaches Illtud's monastery Trynihid notices a grubbily dressed man with a gaunt, unwashed face. He is busy digging a patch of garden. The man is, of course, Illtud himself. However he no longer bears any resemblance to the smart soldier whom Trynihid once married and so she does not recognise him. When she approaches him and tries to strike up a conversation, Illtud ignores her and keeps on digging. She continues to talk – and then suddenly she can no longer see. Illtud has blinded her as a punishment for daring to come and see him.

In the end the angry saint relents and prays that his wife's sight may be restored. It is, but she is not allowed to go away completely unscathed. For the rest of her life the skin of her face is strangely pale, as though she is suffering from some kind of leprosy. Broken in spirit Trynihid goes back to her hermitage in the hills and, perhaps not surprisingly, never approaches her husband again.

It's something of a relief to be able to stress that there is no historical basis for these stories about Illtud's inhuman treatment of his wife. The earliest references and most reliable references to Illtud make no mention of his having been married. There is certainly nothing to indicate that he was a brutal woman-hater. Trynihid seems to have been a product of the Llantwit biographer's fertile and possibly rather unpleasant imagination. Her creation reflects the bitter struggle concerning clerical celibacy that was going on in the twelfth-century church in Wales.

The pre-Norman Welsh church was tribal and nepotistic. Preserving the power of its ecclesiastical Taffia involved a laid back attitude towards married clergy. Clerical dynasties abounded. For example Rhygyfarch of Llanbadarn Fawr, the author of the *Life of St David*, was the eldest of the four sons of Bishop Sulien of St Davids, all of whom are believed to have become priests. Rhygyfarch's brother Daniel (who died in 1127) was Archdeacon of Powys and Daniel's son Cydifor (who died in 1163) became Archdeacon of Cardigan. Lifris of Llancarfan, the Archdeacon of Glamorgan who was mentioned earlier, was also a bishop's son. His father Herewald, a Welshman, was Bishop of Llandaff between 1056 and 1104. Herewald was suspended by Anselm, the Norman Archbishop of Canterbury, as a part of his attempt to bring the church in Wales under Norman control.

The Welsh fought a valiant rearguard action against this threat to their ecclesiastical independence. But then Rome suddenly provided the Normans with a powerful instrument which they could use to break up the native dynasties that had so much power and influence in the Welsh church. The Second Lateran Council of 1139 passed a canon which made clerical marriages both unlawful and invalid. It was this action that seems to have inspired the Norman cleric from Llantwit as he conjured up his description of Illtud's awful (and patently unsaintly) treatment of poor Trynihid, his long-suffering wife.

If clerical celibacy was regarded as something new imposed by foreigners the Welsh clergy would never accept it. If, however, it was seen as a praiseworthy practice whose origins lay deep in their religious past it had a better chance of acceptance. Illtud was the greatest of the Glamorgan saints: a scholar whose reputation was still regarded with pride by the native clergy of his area of Wales. Hence the need to portray this pillar of the pre-Norman church as a married man who had firmly and forcefully repudiated his wife on taking holy orders.

Illtud's Llantwit biographer was a skilful propagandist. His dramatic, well-told and colourful story soon lodged itself in the public mind. The description of Trynihid, stark naked with dishevelled hair, was theoretically intended to be repulsive. In fact, of course, like many such images, it had a certain lascivious appeal which meant that the story would be told over and over again.

It seems to have been partially successful in its aim. The powerful clerical dynasties of early medieval Wales disappeared to be replaced for the most part by successions of celibate Normans. At a lower level, however, the campaign to impose celibacy on the clergy was less successful. In remote and mountainous places priests continued to marry, often producing sons who in turn became priests themselves. For example Bishop Richard Davies, a central figure in the Welsh Reformation, was the son of a North Welsh pre-Reformation priest. He was born around the year 1501 to Jonet, wife of Dafydd ap Gronw, curate of Gyffin.

The most lasting result of the story of Trynihid's trials and tribulations was both unintended and unfortunate. Illtud had once been regarded with awe and admiration as 'the refined master of all Britain' and 'of all the Britons the most accomplished in all the Scriptures'. The Norman biographer's fabrications made him seem a callous, misogynistic brute. Which is why the time has now come to remove this unjust stain from the reputation of one of the greatest figures in early Welsh history.

The outlaw bard:
Glyndŵr's 'Song-thrush' on the run
(March/April 2006)

Llanymynech has been a frontier village for many centuries. These days the days the small community is cut in two by the line that separates Wales and England. Its long-established border status is confirmed by a story told about Llanymynech's most famous son: the sixth-century Saint Beuno.

Beuno, whose link with the area is still commemorated by a sacred spring known locally as 'St Benion's Well', was the son of a couple named Bugi and Beren, who lived on the banks of the Afon Hafren (River Severn). He was sent to a monastic school in Gwent to study Scripture and liturgy and prepare for ordination to the priesthood. Having completed his education, he founded a monastery of his own at what is now Llanfeuno, in the Ewyas region of modern Herefordshire.

It was there that he received a message that his father was seriously ill. Hurrying north to Llanymynech, he arrived in time to administer the last rites to the dying Bugi. After the old man had duly been interred, Beuno planted an acorn by his grave. In time this grew into an enormous oak tree. One of its branches curved down making a kind of archway. The tradition grew up that any Englishman who was rash enough to go through this arch would immediately drop down dead, while any Welshman who went through it would be completely unharmed. There is no record of any courageous Englishman having tested the truth or otherwise of this legend.

Before the Act of Union between England and Wales in 1536, Llanymynech acquired a degree of notoriety. This was because of the Y Graig Lwyd (now known as the White Rock), a wooded outcrop above the village. In Roman times it had attracted lead and copper miners, but by the Middle Ages it had become the haunt of bandits and outlaws. They found it a convenient place, not only because of its wildness and defensibility, but also because it was not subject to English law. They could slip over the border to raid the prosperous Shropshire lowlands, and then skip back home to the safety of their Welsh retreat.

Perhaps the most famous of those who used Y Graig Lwyd as a safe haven was the outlawed poet Llywelyn ab y Moel. He was a descendant of Brochwel Ysgithrog or 'Tusky' Brochwel, the early prince of Powys now best remembered for his kindness and generosity towards St Melangell, the refugee Irish princess. Brochwel's descendants became poets. Llywelyn's father and grandfather, Moel y Pantri and Maredudd Benwyn, were both notable bards. His son, Owain ab Llywelyn ab y Moel, also followed the family calling.

Although Llywelyn came originally from Arwystli in western Powys (or western Montgomeryshire), he had strong family links with the border area. His mother, who could also trace her family tree back to the dentally challenged Brochwel, came from Meifod and some of his other relations held land around Llanymynech at the end of the fourteenth century. When Llywelyn was outlawed it was thus natural enough for him to think of Y Graig Lwyd as a possible hiding place.

The activities that put him beyond the law stemmed from the exciting period into which he was born. There has been a considerable amount of scholarly discussion about the bard's date of birth. 1395 now seems the most likely suggestion. Llywelyn died in February 1440. This meant that his childhood coincided with Owain Glyndŵr's rebellion, and as a headstrong teenager he became caught up in the revolt. His reputation as one of Glyndŵr's enthusiastic supporters was such that, in an elegy written after Llywelyn's death, Guto'r Glyn referred to him as '*bronfraith Owain*' ('Owain's song-thrush'). This is particularly striking because of Llywelyn's youth at the time of the uprising.

Owain Glyndŵr took up arms against Lord Grey of Ruthin in September 1400. At that time Llywelyn was still a small boy. No doubt he spent his childhood listening to stories about Owain's victories, as the Lord of Glyndyfrdwy established himself as the true Prince of Wales. Then grimmer news arrived, as Owain's rebellion began to fall apart. By 1409 the national ruler had become a guerrilla leader, hiding in the hills and launching daring attacks on the English occupying forces whenever possible.

Young Llywelyn might well have sided with the apparent victors. However his patriotic instincts were too deeply rooted for him to think of committing such an act of treachery. Instead he joined the battered army of his hunted hero. What is almost certainly his earliest surviving poem describes the battle of Waun Gaseg. R. Iestyn Daniel, who produced a scholarly edition of Llywelyn's poems in 1998, suggests that this skirmish can be dated to a point between 1410 and Owain Glyndŵr's death in 1416, with the likelihood being that it comes from the beginning of that period..

The fight took place near Abaty Cwm-hir in Radnorshire. The abbey had apparently been garrisoned by troops from Usk who had sided with the English, and were being used to pacify a part of Wales that easily lent itself to guerrilla warfare. Llywelyn and his companions were attempting to dislodge them. A traditional part of a poet's duty in times of war was to sing an impromptu song to raise the spirits of his fellow soldiers before they went into battle. In his poem Llywelyn refers to this. It seems fair to infer that he himself was the one who performed the task. Indeed he may have been deliberately recruited by the war-band to fulfil this function.

Despite Llywelyn's morale-boosting efforts the men of Usk put Owain's followers to flight. The poet remarks how

> It was painful to see, I'm a witness,
> At Waun Gaseg, spears left unused,
> The anguish of our men in the grass…

This traumatic episode not only taught the teenage poet about the realities of war, but also represented the failure of one of the final attempts to rekindle the flames of revolt. Llywelyn and the other survivors were forced to flee northwards, finding refuge in well-established bandit hideouts like Cefn Digoll (the Long Mountain) east of Welshpool and Y Graig Lwyd.

His account of the battle is however especially significant as it is one of only two surviving Welsh poetic descriptions of battles during Owain Glyndŵr's uprising. The prominent poets who had been keen to flatter the Lord of Sycharth and Glyndyfrdwy during the years before 1400, became strangely silent once the revolt began. It may be, of course, that they did indeed compose poems of praise to the new Prince of Wales, but then carefully destroyed them once his cause began to falter. Poets were the PR men and spin-doctors of medieval Wales, and they tended to react swiftly and pragmatically to political changes. A young idealistic bard like Llywelyn ab y Moel was less likely to be tempted to shed his allegiances so quickly.

As a result of his continuing loyalty to Owain Glyndŵr, Llywelyn became an outlaw. Fortunately his family connections with Llanymynech made Y Graig Lwyd an attractive hiding place. His poem to the birch grove may refer to a familiar corner of his wooded refuge. It was composed during a spell of cold March weather, before the trees had come back into leaf. Llywelyn describes the naked birches as 'the spears of Owain's best men'. Although he complains about feeling frozen, the poet is still able to look forward to the summer months when the grove will be a wonderful place for him to canoodle secretly with Euron, his girlfriend.

Llywelyn spent several years among the outlaws of Y Graig Lwyd. Most of his companions were also staunch supporters of Glyndŵr. In a poem in praise of his rocky sanctuary Llywelyn describes the wooded hill above Llanymynech as a city swarming with followers of the defeated Prince:

> A broad sky above the hiding place,
> You are the London of Owain's people,
> A grove of trees full of outlaws,
> Broader than the field of the moon or seas.

This island of Welshness survived as one place where the writ of the English authorities still did not run. Even after Owain's death in 1416 the outlaws of Y Graig Lwyd still held out, transferring their allegiance to his son Maredudd.

One of the ways in which this community kept itself going was by kidnapping wealthy individuals from the other side of the border. In a cheerfully Wenglish phrase Llywelyn refers to '*ransymiaw Sais*' ('ransoming an Englishman'). He also remarks that for a man who wants the good things of this world 'taking an Englishman and despoiling him of his clothes and arms' is far more satisfactory than trying to live on the meagre earnings of a travelling poet.

Llywelyn calls this outpost of lawlessness as '*fy mharadwys*' ('my paradise'). He clearly felt very much at home there. Another money raising activity mentioned in one of his poems is raiding into English territory. The prosperous Shropshire manor of Ruyton-XI-Towns seems to have been a particularly lucrative target.

By 1419, however, even Y Graig Lwyd was no longer a safe place. Owain's remaining supporters in North Wales submitted to the English authorities, and two years later Maredudd ab Owain made peace with Henry V. Llywelyn was thus left in an extremely vulnerable position: penniless, politically suspect and of no fixed abode. He consoled himself by composing a self-pityingly humorous dialogue poem addressed to his purse. Other Welsh poets who had fallen on hard times had done the same. No doubt he sang the poem in sympathetic company, perhaps in wayside inns or in the homes of former supporters of Owain Glyndŵr, and received a free meal or a drink in payment.

As the years went by Llywelyn seems to have gradually settled down to the conventional life of a professional poet. He became involved in a famous poetic disputation with a bardd from Gwynedd, Rhys Goch Eryri. Rhys had written an elegy to the great Powys poet Gruffudd Llwyd, who was notable not only for writing in praise of Owain Glyndŵr, but also as the author of some of the most remarkable Welsh religious poetry of the Middle Ages. Llywelyn took offence at Rhys' poem. It has been suggested that the version that he heard may have had a couple of significant lines omitted. Whether or not this is true, Llywelyn decided that the Gwynedd bard had insulted the poets of Powys, and rushed to defend them. Rhys then explained that there had been a misunderstanding, and the two poets were reconciled.

A poem that can be safely dated to 1433 suggests that the totally changed political situation had finally forced Llywelyn to abandon the position that he had adopted with such enthusiasm in his youth. He addresses extravagant praise to Sir Wiliam ap Tomas of Raglan, 'The Blue Knight of Gwent', the leading supporter of the English Crown in South-East Wales, and the son-in-law of Dafydd Gam, Owain Glyndŵr's most bitter Welsh enemy. It seems hard to condemn him for this. A poet without patrons would soon starve to death, and the Wales of the 1430s was a world away from the glorious dreams of Owain Glyndŵr and the lawless 'paradise' above Llanymynech.

Nevertheless he returned to the Powys borderland for the closing scene of his life. Guto'r Glyn's wonderful *marwnad* (elegy) to Llywelyn describes how the poet had received the last rites from Griffri, one of the monks of Ystrad Marchell, the Cistercian abbey on the banks of the River Severn a few miles south of Y Graig Lwyd. Guto wrote:

> His body became a religious,
> It shall be Mary's anchorite in the choir.
> His soul shall take a new poem
> To the highest heaven.
> My God invited him to the feast,
> And his gift is heaven!

Llywelyn's son Owain would make his living composing poems in praise of the minor gentry of the area around Ystrad Marchell, including several Welsh-speaking patrons on the Shropshire side of the border. Owain ap Llywelyn ab y Moel was a competent poetic craftsman serving a useful social function, but his work contains nothing to equal the excitement of the poetry written by his outlawed father.

'No desert place':
portrait of a Celtic church

(Autumn 1997)

In April 1889 the rector of the Carmarthenshire parish of Brechfa sat at his desk penning a large number of begging letters. The Reverend David Morris Jones politely and diffidently requested 'a little help towards building a new Church for this poor Welsh mountainous parish.' His combination of directness, pathos and courtesy proved remarkably successful. The money poured in. David Morris Jones built his new church and it was duly consecrated by the Bishop of St David's on November 21st 1893. The rector himself, worn out by fund-raising, died almost exactly two years later.

A feature of the building was its three substantial Celtic crosses: one on the bell-cote, a second above the chancel step and the third above the sanctuary. They gave a clear message to anyone who looked up at them: "This is a Celtic Church." It was a bold statement for a Welsh Anglican to make at the time. Disestablishment was on the horizon, and the Church in Wales was the subject of colourful and savage abuse. It was described as an alien church: *'Yr hen estrones'* ('the old foreign woman), and derided as a spiritual dustbin fit only for *'Saeson a phechaduriaid'* ('Englishmen and sinners'). David Morris Jones' Celtic crosses made a different claim. They expressed his belief that his church, far from being an estrones, was in fact *'Yr hen Fam'* ('The old Mother') – the mother church of the people of Wales with its spiritual roots in the age of the Celtic saints.

That assertion became increasingly significant once the Disestablishment Act had been passed. The newly constituted Church in Wales sought its identity in the distant past. One of its leaders proclaimed: "Before Canterbury we were here." The First World War caused a hiatus between the passing of the Act and its implementation. It was during this period of limbo that the little church in Brechfa received a stained glass window which reinforced the message of the three Celtic crosses.

It was given in memory of Squire John William Gwynne-Hughes of Fforest Brechfa and Tregib. In local folk-lore he is best remembered for his vigorous pursuit of village maidens at the annual rent supper in the Forest Arms. His generosity to both church and chapel may have been an attempt to atone for such periodic lapses. The window portrays the risen Christ, with St John the Baptist on his left and St Teilo on his right. Teilo is dressed as a bishop with a crozier in one hand and a gospel-book in the other. Once again there is a message for the *eglwyswyr* (church people) of Brechfa: "You are the spiritual descendants of St Teilo who brought the Gospel of Jesus Christ to this parish in the sixth century."

In the years since disestablishment, and especially during the last quarter century or so, that process of developing a Christian community which draws on roots that stretch back to the beginnings of Christianity in West Wales has continued.

Every August *Gŵyl Sant Teilo a'r Afallennau* – 'The feast of St Teilo and the apple-trees' – is celebrated. The Book of Llandaff records that St Teilo and St Samson planted a substantial orchard in Brittany. The Bretons regard Teilo as the patron saint of apple-trees, and the area around the church which he founded at Landeleau is still produces excellent cider. The Brechfa version of the Breton festival is a cheerfully quadrilingual occasion which includes decorating the church with apple-branches, performing a miracle play about St Teilo's exploits in Brittany, blessing the apple-trees in the churchyard, and singing a song, the chorus of which (in the English version) is as follows:

> Teilo, a kindly man was he,
> He went from Brechfa to Brittany.
> He rescued the Bretons from their misery,
> And then he planted an apple-tree.

A hundred years after David Morris Jones put Celtic crosses on his new church the church folk of Brechfa have come to see themselves as a part of *'Teulu Teilo'* – Teilo's family.

It might be argued that this attempt to draw inspiration from the 'Age of Saints' represents a triumph of imagination over historical reality. Yet there are real continuities which make it possible to develop a genuine expression of Celtic spirituality in such a parish. The Black Book of Carmarthen, the thirteenth-century manuscript which contains the earliest surviving collection of religious poetry written in West Wales, includes the lovely lines:

> On hills, in valleys, on the islands of the sea,
> Wherever you may go,
> Because of holy Christ there is no desert place.

The medieval Welsh Triads describe Dewi, Teilo and Padarn, the three great sixth-century Christian leaders in West Wales, as 'The Three Blessed Visitors of the Island of Britain'. It was they and their contemporaries who ensured that even the remotest Welsh valley was 'no desert place'.

Over 1400 years ago Teilo came to Brechfa: the triangle of land where the little rivers Pib and Marlais come together to flow into the Cothi. He planted his staff in the ground by the spring which supplied the people of the area with their drinking water, and rang his silver bell to call them to listen to him. He preached and prayed and baptized and gave communion, and one of his priests (perhaps chosen from among his new converts) remained to care for the new Christian tribe or extended family. And despite all sorts of ups and downs across the centuries that community is still there in the 'poor Welsh mountainous parish' which Teilo made his own.

Teilo's converts were baptized with water from what became known as Ffynnon Deilo ('St Teilo's Spring'). In recent years the watercourse has been disturbed and the spring has dried up. Today all that remains of the ancient holy well is a muddy patch and a little wall, hidden away in a corner of the village park. However water from Ffynnon Deilo was used for every baptism in Brechfa from the sixth century until mains water came to the village in the 1950s. There's something very powerful about sacramental continuity in one small spot over so many centuries, particularly when the water used as a sign of spiritual life comes from the same source which quenches the everyday thirst of the community.

There is a continuity of worship as well. David Gwenallt Jones expressed his understanding of the Christian belief in the Communion of Saints in a poem to Dewi Sant (St David):

> There is no border between two worlds in the Church;
> The Church militant on earth is one
> With the victorious Church in Heaven.
> And the saints will be in the two-one Church.
> They come to worship with us, a little congregation,
> The saints, our oldest ancestors,
> Who built Wales on the basis of
> The Crib, the Cross and the Empty Grave...

Gwenallt's lines do not only speak of continuity of worship. They also emphasis a shared faith which the poet regards as the foundation of the nation itself. The Crib, the Cross and the Empty Grave – Christmas, Good Friday and Easter – Incarnation, Atonement and Resurrection – this fundamental pattern of the Christian year and Christian teaching provides a spiritual rhythm to life that is intended to sanctify time itself. In rural West Wales it was the *eglwyswyr* – the church people – who preserved this pattern through the centuries.

The traditional nonconformity of the area had little time for the major Christian festivals. Elfed (the Reverend H. Elvet Lewis), the greatest hymnwriter among the *Annibynwyr* (Welsh Independents), described the attitude to Christmas in Cynwyl Elfed, Carmarthenshire, during his childhood in the late 1860s and early 1870s:

> There was no Christmas in the neighbourhood where I was brought up some eighty years ago. It was in the Almanac and that was about it. A sort of half holiday and half work day. Idling – and giving up. Working – and giving up. That was Christmas...

But in the church *Y Plygain* was celebrated before dawn on Christmas morning. In north and mid Wales this is essentially a carol service. In west Wales, however, it is always a Communion Service: the Mass of the Shepherds, who come to greet the Christ-child in the stable in Bethlehem before the break of day.

Changing patterns of rural life and the falling number of clergy have meant that Plygain in its original form at its traditional time has almost vanished from rural west Wales. In Brechfa it is still celebrated at 6am every Christmas. One sheep farmer told me that his father had always said "You should never miss the *Plygain* – it is the most important service of all." Someone else remembered how, some 70 or more years ago, an *eglwyswr* had married a chapel girl and stopped going to *Plygain*. "All the lads from the church went round to his house after the service and sang hymns under his window so that he couldn't sleep. The next year he got up and joined them for the *Plygain*." One woman described how, between the two World Wars, she and her mother used to walk several miles to the *Plygain* at Brechfa Church.

Perhaps the most famous of the north Welsh *Plygain* carols, written by Eos Iâl (Dafydd Hughes), echoes the verses in St Paul's letter to the Philippians, which describe how Christ emptied himself of his majesty by being born among us as one of us:

> Christ took off his crown, of his free will,
> That he might crown Zion of his free will;
> Bending his undefiled head
> Under the crown of thorns,
> To suffer angry scorn, of his free will,
> To raise the guilty's head, of his free will.

This loving humility of God in Christ has left its mark on the way of thinking of people in north Carmarthenshire. Perhaps the highest praise that can be given to anyone in a position of power and authority is to say *'Mae e'n isel iawn'* ('He's very lowly' – as opposed to someone who is pompous or arrogant).

As Eos Iâl's carol reminds us, the crib leads to the cross. In Brechfa there is a farm on the edge of the village called Maes-y-groes: 'the field of the cross'. It has been suggested that a wayside cross stood there in the Middle Ages. Local tradition insists that, after the Reformation, the brutal Lords of the Forest of Glyn Cothi used it as a place of execution for those who had fallen foul of their laws. On Good Friday a rough-hewn wooden cross is carried through the village to Maes-y-groes and an open-air service is held in the farmyard there. Calvary and its message have thus become a part of the spiritual geography of the parish.

Beyond the cross is Easter. There are many ways of interpreting the Celtic cross. When Brechfa's lay Eucharistic assistant, a skilled carpenter and cabinet-maker, carved the cross of St Teilo, the solid circle on which the cross was imposed had rays like the sun. He saw the Celtic cross as a symbol of the resurrection: glorious new light and life shining through and because of the cross. That light and life lead to joy and praise. Some other lines from the Black Book of Carmarthen echo down the centuries:

> Hail glorious Lord, may church and chancel praise thee;
> May chancel and church praise thee;
> May plain and mountainside praise thee...

Far away in Lichfield Cathedral lie the Gospels of St Teilo, purloined by greedy English monks around the year 1000. The eighth- and ninth-century writings in its margins contain some of the earliest examples of written Welsh. They also contain the first known refence to Brechfa, as being given to God and St Teilo for ever. A 'poor Welsh mountainous parish' must inevitably be marginal – but there is something to be said for being in the margin of one of the most beautiful Gospel-books ever produced.

A vanished hero

(June/July 2007)

The head waiter in the restaurant on the shores of Lake Sevan in Armenia bore a striking and slightly unnerving resemblance to Councillor Peter Hughes Griffiths, the energetic Plaid Cymru former mayor of Carmarthen. Naira, my guide, introduced me: "This is Patrick. He comes from Wales." The head waiter beamed enthusiastically: "Wales is an ancient country, like Armenia," he said. "We have both had to struggle a long time for our freedom." He showed me to a table, and began to help me to expand my rather limited grasp of Eastern Armenian.

His opening remark struck a chord. I began to think about some of the similarities between our two small mountainous countries. Several religious, artistic, cultural and linguistic parallels had impressed me. But one figure in particular thrust himself into the forefront of my mind: Khachatur Abovian, an Armenian national hero whose name and statue adorn one of the most important streets in Yerevan, the capital.

The hero who mysteriously disappears from sight is a well-established figure in Welsh tradition. The 'Stanzas of the Graves' in *Llyfr Du Caerfyrddin* (The Black Book of Carmarthen) emphasize the mysterious nature of Arthur's grave, while Owain Glyndŵr vanishes into the mists of Pumlumon. It's true that some rather dodgy medieval monks managed to fabricate and then 'discover' Arthur's grave at Glastonbury, while modern enthusiasts have attempted to identify Glyndŵr's last resting place at churchyards in Herefordshire and Carmarthenshire. However, I can't help feeling that both the medieval forgers and the modern historical detectives have missed the point. Some heroes are meant to vanish.

A grave has an air of finality to it. Visiting the place where Llywelyn Ein Llyw Olaf is buried, we feel something of the agony and despair that led Gruffudd ab Yr Ynad Coch to compose his heart-rending *marwnad* on the last Welsh Prince.

Arthur and Owain are different. Because they have disappeared there remains a tantalising possibility that they might reappear. They acquire a quality that dissolves the limitations of linear time. They become eternal figures who can rekindle the spirit of the nation at times when its flame burns low.

Vanishing and returning heroes have an aura of myth about them. The Armenian national folk epic, *David of Sassoun*, a cycle of oral sagas composed in the far distant past, but not written down until the nineteenth century, ends with the disappearance of Mher and his horse into the Rock of Van. Each year on Transfiguration and Ascension Day the rider and his mount emerge and gallop around Armenia at great speed for forty days assessing the state of the land. It is said that one day a shepherd found the entrance to Mher's Rock open and went in. He saw the hero, and asked when he would be free from his imprisonment. Mher replied that that would only happen when the world ceased to be evil and its soil became abundantly fruitful.

Khachatur Abovian, however, comes from a rather different background to that medieval folk hero. He belongs to the Transcaucasian fringe of the Romantic nationalism that swept across Europe in the opening decades of the nineteenth century. Abovian was born at Kanaker near Yerevan in Eastern Armenia (then a part of Persia) in 1809. His native village was described by a European visitor as 'a most agreeable spot, situate on the slope of the fertile and beautiful Gokchai Mountains... It enjoys a clear, mild and salubrious atmosphere, and ...commands one of the most beautiful views of Ararat...' Mount Ararat (Mount Massis) is to Armenians what Snowdon (Yr Wyddfa) is to us in Wales: a national symbol and a source of spiritual and poetic inspiration, There is an added poignancy attached to Ararat because, although it is visible from much of Armenia, it is now in Turkey, and the border between the two countries is closed. It can be seen by Armenians, but no longer reached by them. This sacred mountain was to play a crucial role in Khachatur Abovian's life.

In 1819 the young boy was sent from Kanaker to Holy Etchmiadzin, the spiritual centre of the Armenians. A special altar in the Cathedral there marks the place where, at the beginning of the fourth century, Christ appeared in a vision to St Grigor Lusavorich, the country's patron saint. Abovian began his education under the wing of the religious community there and then in 1822 had the opportunity to continue his studies in the Georgian capital of Tiflis (Tbilisi). There he became one of the first pupils in the Nersessian Academy, where, among other subjects, he studied Armenian, Russian and Persian.

In 1826 war broke out between Persia and Russia. The Armenians fought courageously alongside the Russians, who had promised them a state of their own. By 1828, when the war concluded with a treaty that awarded Eastern Armenia to the Russians, the victors had conveniently forgotten their pledge. Abovian had dreamed of studying in Europe, but by 1829 he was back in Etchmiadzin, a deacon destined for a life of service to the church. His personal situation and that of his betrayed country left him in a state of profound despair.

Then something quite unexpected happened that was to transform his life. Professor Friedrich Parrot, a German naturalist from the University of Dorpat (Tartu) in what was then Baltic Russia and is now Estonia., arrived in Etchmiadzin on an expedition to reach the summit of Mount Ararat. Because Abovian was fluent in Russian, the Catholicos (the head of the Armenian Church) selected him to be Parrot's guide and interpreter.

Armenian Christians regarded Ararat as a sacred mountain that was impossible to climb. They repeated the legend of St Jacob of Nisibis, who had made the attempt many centuries before in the hope of discovering the remains of Noah's Ark. Jacob would climb part of the mountain each day and then settle down for the night. Every morning he would wake up and find himself back in the exact place from which he had set off the day before. Eventually an angel took pity on him and gave him a fragment of the wood of the Ark. The saint abandoned his climb and took the relic to Holy Etchmiadzin, where it is still treasured and shown to visitors.

Parrot was impressed by his young companion, remarking of Abovian that 'he established a claim for our respect and gratitude by his earnest thirst after knowledge, his modesty, self-denial and pious feelings, no less than by his penetration, his courage and his perseverance.' For Abovian the ascent of Ararat was a profound spiritual experience. He knew that he would have to face scepticism from the fellow members of his religious community. The deacon erected crosses on and near the summit, at points where they might provide visible proof of the success of the expedition. He also filled a flask with ice from the top of Ararat, later presenting it to his religious superiors.

This does not seem to have deflected the hostility that met him on his return from the mountain. He was persecuted mercilessly by his fellow monks Fortunately Professor Parrot had not forgotten his youthful Armenian guide. He obtained a scholarship for Abovian, enabling him to travel to the Baltic and study at the University of Dorpat, where he encountered the mainstream of European culture. Writers who had a profound influence on his thought and literary development were Goethe, Rousseau and Sir Walter Scott. However his interest in other languages and literatures did not lessen Abovian's deep love and concern for his mother tongue. He would later tell his young Armenian readers: 'Learn ten languages – but keep your own language and faith alive.'

In 1836 Abovian returned to the Armenian community in Tiflis filled with an intense desire to transform the future of his people. He threw himself into teaching. The ecclesiastical establishment had treated him with suspicion and hostility, and so in 1839 he turned his back on his monastic vocation and married a German wife. In 1843 they moved to Yerevan. Abovian had been appointed director of studies of the provincial school there.

His reforming educational ideas would have an important impact on the future of his country, but even more significant was his attitude towards its language. Classical Armenian was the product of the fifth century 'Golden Age' of Armenian literature. It was the language of the Bible and the Church Liturgy and was the medium of instruction in schools. Unfortunately the Armenian tongue had evolved and changed to such an extent over the centuries that the ancient literary language was incomprehensible to all but its keenest devotees.

One of the lessons which Abovian had learnt during his time in Dorpat was the innate link between language and national identity. He decided that his country needed a written language that could be understood by ordinary people. The everyday Armenian of his childhood was rich in idioms and perceptive turns of phrase. Drawing on it, he shaped modern Eastern Armenian into a medium for literature. He showed what was possible by writing *The Wounds of Armenia*, the first Eastern Armenian novel, based on the events of the war between Russia and Persia.

By 1848 the 39-year-old teacher and writer had amassed an impressive portfolio of achievements. He was the first Armenian to scale the iconic mountain of Ararat and the first Armenian to graduate from a European university. He had introduced progressive ideas which, through the influence of his pupils, would eventually transform Armenia's schools and colleges. He had also laid the foundations of a modern Armenian literature that would develop and deepen the self-understanding and self-respect of his people. And then, early in the morning of 2 April 1848 Khachatur Abovian left his home in Yerevan and disappeared.

What happened to him? Two possibilities have been put forward by those who have attempted to solve the mystery. One is that the Russian Tsarist secret police, suspicious of his nationalistic activities, quietly kidnapped Abovian and spirited him away to Siberia. Attempts to find concrete evidence of this have so far been unsuccessful. The other theory is that Abovian committed suicide. There is certainly evidence from his writings that, like many creative people, he experienced bouts of severe and even suicidal depression. However most of the references to these periods of despair date from his time in Dorpat, when he was cut off from family and friends and worried about whether he would pass his exams. If he did indeed kill himself, his body was never found.

An ending that somehow seems more appropriate to those of us brought up on stories of Y Brenin Arthur and Owain Glyndŵr was offered to me during a visit to the exhibition room of the Matenadaran, the Institute of Armenian Manuscripts in Yerevan. Among the treasures on display there is the original letter, signed by the Catholicos, giving Khachatur Abovian permission to scale Mount Ararat. "One day Abovian climbed Mount Ararat and vanished … " remarked the guide as she showed us the ornate document . Which conjured up in my mind a picture of the courageous writer struggling back up the holy mountain that had brought him both suffering and fame – and disappearing into the layer of mist which often makes the peaks of Ararat seem to float freely in the air.

Perhaps one day, when Mount Ararat is restored to Armenia, Khachatur Abovian will reappear in his homeland. In the meantime we in our small country can draw inspiration from his dedication to his people and their language and culture, and his determination that, against at times what seemed insuperable odds, their nation would survive.

*Those who are interested in learning more about Abovian and his work should try to track down **Khatchadour Abovian et La Renaissance Litteraire en Armenie Orientale** by Hrant Adjemian (Antelias, Lebanon,1986) and **Khachatur Abovyan – The Preface to Wounds of Armenia: Lamentation of a Patriot**, introduced by Vahé Baladouni (Yerevan, 2005).*

Finding Nancy Caepandy:
places and people in *cefn gwlad Cymru*
(August/September 2006)

"You really must go and visit Nancy Caepandy," my predecessor advised me during my first week as rector of a group of deeply rural north Carmarthenshire parishes. I scanned the list of church members and was baffled. There was no 'Nancy' on it and no 'Caepandy' either. It took quite a bit of careful questioning (*'holi mas'* as the local dialect calls it) to discover that Nancy was in fact officially 'Mrs Esther Davies' and that 'Caepandy' had been renamed as 'Forest Lodge' some time before the Second World War. Mind you, the visit was certainly worthwhile. Nancy, a cheerful, generous-hearted woman, makes what is probably the finest *tarten 'fale* (apple pie) in Wales (if not the world).

Before the English came we tended to carry our ancestry around with us, adding in the occasional nickname: *'Fychan'* if someone was particularly short, *'Foel'* if he was noticeably bald or *'Goch'* if he had a bushy red beard. Anglo-Saxon administrative tidiness, however, could not cope with a name like Maelgwn Fychan ap Maelgwn ap Rhys (after all, what letter would you file it under?). The family trees were therefore lopped and most people were left with a single surname, usually in an Anglicized form. That created its own inconvenience, as anyone looking for a John Jones in the Swansea telephone directory quickly discovers. In rural Wales the solution to the problem was traditionally solved by a combination of local geography and personal history.

Take, for example, the late Mr John Thomas, another of my valued parishioners up in the hills. John began his life at a house in Brechfa named Union Hall, and therefore his old school-friends and those who had known him in his childhood naturally called him 'John Union Hall'. Later he moved to Derwendeg, also in the village – so to others he was 'John Derwendeg'. He got a job artificially inseminating cattle, and thus became 'John A.I.' to those who knew him in a professional capacity. By the time that I arrived in the parish he had moved to Plasparke, just above the village, and so I tended to think of him as 'John Plasparke'. He ended his days in one of the old people's bungalows, which a previous occupant had cosily named 'Clydfan' – and, in his declining years, one or two sticklers for accuracy insisted on talking about 'John Clydfan'. Such a range of surnames has a huge potential for confusing those who are not in the know, and can only flourish in a close-knit, comparatively stable community.

Coming into such communities from outside can be challenging. When I arrived in the Cardiganshire parish of Gartheli, my churchwardens insisted that my first and most important visit should be to *'Anti Jên Emporium'*, the matriarch of the church. The word 'emporium' suggested a rather grand shop. I searched high and low for such an establishment in Llwyn-y-groes, the main village. All I could find was a post office, which also sold a few groceries and odds and ends. It was run by a couple of newcomers from England. They were quite delightful, but were clearly not the person I was looking for. Footsore and despairing, I eventually found myself in front of a small, old-fashioned-looking cottage. Peering at the peeling sign attached to the rickety wooden gate, I could just make out the name 'Emporium'. A few moments later I was sitting by an ancient grate on which a large kettle was boiling, having a chat with the remarkable Mrs Jane Davies. It turned out that the name 'Emporium' was the result of a trip to the seaside by an inhabitant of Llwyn-y-groes somewhere in the distant past. Dazzled by the wonders of Aberystwyth the visitor had noticed the word 'Emporium' on a shop sign, and decided that it would make a delightful name for his home.

A tendency to extravagant nomenclature seems to have been part of the Gartheli tradition. The parish hall was always referred to as 'Athen' (Athens), although the only seat of learning that it had ever housed was the church school. It was there that Jane Emporium received her education, and was taught the beautiful Welsh in which she used to pen the occasional scathing letter to the vicar, if she felt that he had been neglecting his duties (the elegance of the language made up for the vitriol of her sentiments). In fact Gartheli had a distinguished intellectual heritage. One of the sons of the tiny church was Dr John Davies, Hendre-Phylip, a leading nineteenth-century philosopher and author of *The Estimate of the Human Mind*, who ended up as a Canon of Durham Cathedral. His daughter founded Girton College, Cambridge, and his son, a fellow of King's College, Cambridge, was also a champion of higher education for women. Jane Davies, Emporium, shared their razor-sharp intellect, but lacked their opportunities to develop it.

That the English word 'Emporium' should have been given to a house in a Welsh community at a time when little or no English was spoken there reflects not only a delight in words for their own sake, but also an era when language had not yet become a battleground. Another linguistic inconsistency could be found in the attractive Carmarthenshire village of Abergorlech. Many chapels have a *tŷ capel* attached to them. It's often the house where the chapel cleaner or caretaker lives. Capel Newydd, Abergorlech, is a bastion of Cymreictod – a Welsh-language chapel in the old tradition of the Carmarthenshire *Annibynwyr* (Independents). Yet, for some long-forgotten reason, its *tŷ capel* became known as 'Chapel House'. And when I was appointed Vicar of Abergorlech the person who lived in Chapel House was a staunch *Eglwyswr* ('Churchman'/Anglican).

It was only some years later, when Edwin Chapel House was unexpectedly taken into hospital, that I suddenly realised that I had no idea what his official surname was (it turned out to be 'Jones'). Everyone in Abergorlech Church knew him as 'Yr Hen Chapel House' – and there was a famous and oft-repeated anecdote that made him very much a part of the church's history. There used to be a tradition in many Welsh country churches that the women and men would go up to the altar rail separately to receive Holy Communion. The women would go first, and then the men. A new squire came to the local *plas*, who either was unaware of this ancient custom (which may well go back to the time of Dewi Sant), or else was determined to ignore it. On his first Sunday in the parish he arrived at the village church in all his finery, and, when the summons to Communion came, strode down the aisle to receive the Sacrament before anyone else.

Chapel House was appalled by what he regarded as an arrogant and outrageous insult to the women of the church. He decided that the new squire needed to be taken down a peg or two. At the time Edwin was working in the forestry and he recruited one of his fellow workers to join him. Before the service they crept into church and squatted down out of sight in a pew at the front of the church. The service began. The priest called the congregation forward to Communion, and the squire began his majestic progress down the aisle. Before he had even reached the chancel step, Edwin and his workmate had darted forward from their hiding-place and were kneeling devoutly at the altar-rail. The squire was appalled to see such riff-raff in front of him, but he had no choice but to kneel down beside them. He never came to Communion in Abergorlech Church again, going instead to the genteel stronghold of Llandeilo, where he was sure that he would receive the respect which he felt that members of the gentry deserved.

This radical streak may have been a reflection of Edwin's background in industrial South Wales. He was an orphan who had been brought up in one of Doctor Barnardo's homes and then, as was the custom at that time, sent out as a young lad to work as cheap labour on a farm. Coming to the Abergorlech area he quickly became fluent in Welsh and, after a period as a forestry worker, became a lengthsman in charge of maintaining a stretch of rural road. Welsh humour contains countless jokes about the inactivity of '*bois yr heol*', but in Edwin's case such a slur was certainly undeserved. He became renowned for the conscientiousness with which he cared for his precious section of the highway.

His other love was singing. Abergorlech Church had a *codwr canu* to start the singing on those occasions when the organist was unable to be there. Edwin was appointed to this post, and took to it with enthusiasm. Every Sunday he would set out from Chapel House to the church with his treasured sol-fa edition of *Emynau'r Eglwys*, the church hymnbook, tucked carefully under his arm. A non-church-going Englishman moved into the house next door. He was working in his garden one Sunday morning when he spotted the old *codwr canu* setting off for the *cwrdd*. "Say one for me, Edwin!" he called out cheerily. Edwin had no time for what the sociologists now like to call 'vicarious religion'. "Certainly not," he answered sternly. "You can paddle your own canoe across the Jordan!"

In 1985 Bishop George Noakes (later to be Archbishop of Wales) visited Abergorlech to conduct a service that marked the centenary of the restoration and rededication of the church. Someone took a photograph of the *codwr canu* and the future Archbishop deep in conversation. It became Edwin Chapel House's most valued possession, and when ill-health forced him to leave the village and move into an old people's home in Carmarthen, he insisted that I should bring him two things: his well-thumbed hymnbook and the photograph, which he hung on the wall of his room.

Chapel House has been sold long ago. It's possible that it may have a new name by now. For me, however, the old name will always conjure up the memory of a small but stout-hearted man, with an ancient hat on his head, a woollen muffler round his neck and a hymnbook under his arm. Because of the way in which a particular spot was linked with a particular individual in the characteristic Welsh rural way of naming people, person and place acquired a profoundly significant connection. Life in *cefn gwlad* was filled with people whose present or former homes had somehow become part of their personality: Jack Maes-y-bwlch, Beti Penybanc, Harold Felin Marlais, John Maes-y-groes...

It's slightly different for clergy. In the beginning one or two of the staider folk addressed me as '*Rheithor*' or '*Ficer*' (I was a rector in one of my parishes, and vicar of the other two). However, as my deservedly much-loved predecessor still lived in the village, he was still the real rector in most people's eyes, so I became 'Tomos' to the older Welsh-speaking people and 'Patrick' to the children and the English-speakers. There was, however, one exception to this. Traditionally people in *cefn gwlad* regard Anglican clergy as being rather dim. The result is that loyal *Eglwyswyr* tend to be a bit defensive about their *ffeiradon*. Because I had a few letters after my name, my loyal parishioners could indulge in occasional one-upmanship, introducing me to chapel people as '*Doctor* Thomas'. However, lest I become too full of myself, I soon discovered that, on less formal occasions, I would be identified as '*ffeirad ni – y boi wiscas coch 'na*' ('our priest – that chap with red whiskers'). I knew that I had really arrived when complete strangers started coming up to me saying "*Ffeirad Brechfa y'ch chi*" ("You're the Brechfa priest"). For a few years I found my own special niche in the mysterious Welsh geography that links person and place. Moving on from there left me feeling strangely rootless and bereft – a not uncommon feeling in our rapidly changing country.

On the death of a prince:
remembering Llywelyn ap Gruffudd

(January/February 2008)

One Autumn afternoon in the early 1970s I was sitting in the library of a Cambridge college, leafing through the *Oxford Book of Welsh Verse*, with a battered grammar and a substantial dictionary at my elbow. A poem suddenly caught my eye: '*Marwnad Llywelyn ap Gruffudd*' by Gruffudd ab yr Ynad Coch. I already knew that a *marwnad* was an elegy, but, at that point, my knowledge of Welsh history was extremely vague. As I slowly attempted to decipher the meaning of the poem, I gradually became aware that its subject was the death of the last native Prince of Wales (apart from Owain Glyndŵr), and that the poet regarded his loss as being of cosmic significance.

The passage which struck most forcefully home contained Gruffudd's series of anguished questions:

> *Poni welwch-chwi hynt y gwynt a'r glaw?*
> *Poni welwch-chwi'r deri yn ymdaraw?*
> *Poni welwch-chwi'r môr yn merwinaw -'r tir?*
> *Poni welwch-chwi'r gwir yn ymgweiriaw?*
> *Poni welwch-chwi'r haul yn hwylaw -'r awyr?*
> *Poni welwch-chwi'r sŵr wedi r'syrthiaw?*
> *Poni chredwch-chwi i Dduw, ddyniadon ynfyd?*
> *Poni welwch-chwi'r byd wedi r'bydiaw.*
> *Och hyd atat-ti, Dduw, na ddaw – môr dros dir!*
> *Pa beth y'n gedir i ohiriaw?*

The rain and wind of a Welsh winter storm become increasingly intense, driving the oak trees against one another. The sea lashes the land. The shape of the truth is shifting and re-arranging itself, while the sun careers through the sky from which the stars have fallen. Foolish earthlings are tempted to deny God's existence as the world's future comes into question. The poet asks God why the sea won't pour across the land, so that he and his audience may be wiped out instead of being left to languish in despair.

This expression of cataclysmic disaster pours from the poet's heart. The imagery echoes both the apocalyptic visions of the *Book of Revelation* and the ancient folk-memories of devastating floods in the legend of Cantre'r Gwaelod. As I slowly made out the meaning of Gruffudd's words, with the help of my well-thumbed grammar and dictionary, I became increasingly aware of the horror that he had felt as he found himself caught up in such an overwhelming catastrophe – and with that awareness came a sense of my own lost Welsh identity, and a deep desire to reclaim it.

Gruffudd ab yr Ynad Coch's most recent editors, Rhian M. Andrews and Catherine McKenna, describe his lament on the death of Llywelyn as 'a passionate, dramatic and personal poem, with its emphasis on the awfulness of the present after Llywelyn's fall.' A reference in the poem leads Rhian Andrews to suggest that it was probably composed and sung at Castell y Bere, at some point in the desperate period between Llywelyn's death in December 1282 and the surrender of that last Welsh stronghold at the end of April 1283. Those winter months were a devastating time for those who attempted to prolong the Welsh resistance. The garrison of Castell y Bere were hugely outnumbered, ill-resourced and starving. The poem torn from the depths of Gruffudd's being was a heart-wrenching cry of pain and loss that must have echoed the feelings of his companions.

The poet describes the impact of the death of the 'lion of Nantcoel' and the 'breastplate of Nancaw' on his followers and their families. He sings of tear-stained cheeks, gaping wounds and bloody feet, of screaming widows and minds on the edge of madness, of fatherless children and farms laid waste. In the midst of this catalogue of misery, there is a hint at a disturbing reason for the disaster. Gruffudd mentions '*Llawer llef druan fal ban fu Gamlan*' ('Many a piteous cry, as there was at Camlan').

Llywelyn ap Gruffudd was killed on the banks of the River Irfon on 11 December 1282. Two different men are named in the English chronicles of the period as being responsible for the death of the Welsh prince. Both were Shropshire landowners: Stephen de Frankton and Sir Robert Body. Earlier scholars tended to regard Frankton as the most likely candidate. J. Beverley Smith, however, in his comprehensive and magisterial biography of Llywelyn, points out that Body is identified as the man who killed the prince by Robert Mannyng of Bourne, a Lincolnshire chronicler who may have had access to particularly reliable information. Mannyng was connected with Sempringham, the religious establishment in which Gwenllian, Llywelyn's infant daughter, was confined after the Welsh defeat. Sir Robert Body would go on to join the army besieging Gruffudd ab yr Ynad Coch and his companions in Castell y Bere in 1283.

There is no doubt that one of the Shropshire men killed Llywelyn, but many of the other circumstances surrounding the prince's death are far more difficult to pin down. J. Beverley Smith remarks: 'We shall probably never get to the root of the truth about the final day of the prince of Wales. Was it a sudden accident or a long-intended trick? Was he a lonely fugitive, or with his men in battle?'

There seems to be some evidence of treachery against Llywelyn. Under its entry for 1282, the Welsh chronicle *Brenhinedd y Saesson* contains a mysterious reference to the way in which Llywelyn's own men were responsible for working out his betrayal '*ynghylochdyau Bangor*' ('in the belfries of Bangor'). This certainly appears to suggest there was a plot against the prince, which had its origins in Llywelyn's heartland, and probably involved hostile clerics.

The chronicler goes on to record, at the end of his account of the year, that Llywelyn sent his steward and most of his men 'to receive the homage of the men of Brycheiniog'. The prince, left with a depleted bodyguard, was surprised and killed by the English king's forces, supported by Roger Mortimer and Gruffudd ap Gwenwynwyn. The writer concludes with words which echo the poet's lament: '*Ac yna y bwriwyd holl Gymry i'r llawr*' ('And then all Wales was cast to the ground').

If, as we are tempted to assume, Gruffudd ab yr Ynad Coch was among the beleaguered defenders of Castell y Bere after Llywelyn's death, it is likely that he would have known of the suspicion that treachery might have played a part in that tragedy. His reference to Camlan in his *marwnad* for Llywelyn suggests that he did indeed wish to make his audience aware that some kind of double-dealing had played a part in the events that led up to the killing on the banks of the river Irfon.

Camlan, of course, was the battle between Arthur and his nephew Medrawd. *Trioedd Ynys Prydein* ('The Triads of the Island of Britain'), that handy list of threes that helped to jog the memories of medieval Welsh storytellers, describes it as one of the 'Three Futile Battles of the Island of Britain.' What is significant about those 'Three Futile Battles' is, not so much the apparently rather trivial incidents which were said to have been the original cause of each one, but the fact that they were all battles between Britons and Britons (or Welsh and Welsh, to update the terminology). Medrawd himself is described as the 'third and worst' of the 'Three Dishonoured Men who were in the Island of Britain', because of the way in which he betrayed Arthur. Camlan and disaster caused by treachery were synonymous in the medieval Welsh mind, as Gruffudd ab yr Ynad Coch knew when he referred to the battle in his *marwnad* for Llywelyn.

After betrayal and death came mutilation. When the Cistercian monks of Abaty Cwm Hir kindly and secretly buried Llywelyn's remains, one essential part was missing. The corpse that they buried was without a head, and this had a significance that went far deeper than being merely a reflection of characteristic medieval brutality towards one's enemies. Gruffudd remarks sadly:

> Bychan lles im, am fy nhwyllaw,
> Gadael pen arnaf heb ben arnaw.

('It's not much good for me, deceiving me: leaving my head on, when he is without one.')

He then launches into the climax of his elegy, which focuses on the head that had been cut from Llywelyn's body.

Llywelyn's head was first sent to the English king at Rhuddlan, where it was no doubt the subject of mockery and scorn. Then, in a crafty political move, it was sent to Ynys Môn and displayed to the people of Aberffraw and the surrounding district. One of the problems of politics in a pre-photographic age was that it was often difficult to convince people that a particular ruler had died, especially when his death took place far away from where he normally held court. Most of Llywelyn's subjects in Anglesey knew what their prince looked like. However, a report that he had been killed at the other end of Wales might well have been dismissed by them as an empty rumour or enemy propaganda. Showing them his head was a brutal but effective way of proving that their prince was indeed dead.

They were not permitted to give it a dignified burial. Instead the grisly relic was sent to London, to be put on an iron spike in public view above the Tower of London. There was a particularly cruel refinement to this final exhibition. The battered, decaying head was crowned with ivy, as a deliberate and scornful commentary on the oft-repeated Welsh prophecy that one day someone of the ancient British lineage would be crowned in London. Back in north Wales Gruffudd could only speak of his horror that an iron pole now pierced *'pen Llywelyn deg'* ('the head of fair Llywelyn').

For the pre-Christian Celts the head had a special and sacred significance as a source of power. The heads of ancestors were venerated and the heads of enemies were coveted. Archaeologists have come across relics of this practice in the Roman city of Wroxeter, which would later be a part of the post-Roman principality of the unfortunate Cynddylan. Elements of the pagan head-cult were absorbed into early Welsh Christianity. Perhaps the most famous example is a skull from pre-Christian times that was re-branded as the 'skull of St Teilo' and carefully guarded for centuries by the Melchior family of Llandeilo Llwydiarth in Pembrokeshire, who allowed people to use it to scoop water from the sacred spring there. Echoes of the head-cult are also particularly strong in the life of St Beuno, who on several occasions put back the head of someone who had been decapitated, restoring them to life.

A poem which reflects the particular significance of a prince's head is included in an early cycle of Welsh verses that may once have been part of a saga about the Cumbrian hero Urien Rheged. Urien had been killed at a place called Aber Lleu and his body buried in an oak coffin beneath earth and stones. Before his burial, however, his corpse had been decapitated, not by his enemies, but by his friends. The poem *'Pen Urien'* ('Urien's head') is a lament put in the mouth of one his faithful, broken-hearted followers, as he rides along with his dead prince's head in a bag at his side. His actions suggest that, at the time the verses were written, the head of a prince who had been a great warrior was seen as having a lasting protective power, which meant that it should not be allowed to fall into enemy hands.

That is also the message conveyed by the most famous Welsh head of all: that of Bendigeidfran, in the Second Branch of the *Mabinogion*. The giant's head was taken London to be buried, sorrowfully and respectfully, under the Gwynfryn, facing France, to protect the Island of the Mighty from invasion. Llywelyn's head was taken to the Tower built on that same Gwynfryn, but instead of being treated with honour and used as a symbol of protection, the Welsh prince's head became the focus of mockery and a sign of the Saxon oppressor's victory. There was an agonizing irony there of which Gruffudd ab yr Ynad Coch was only too aware.

Dreaming of Cambriol:
William Vaughan's New Wales
(May/June 1999)

There are many maps of Wales, Cymru or Cambria. There is only one map of Cambriol. In 1625 an engraving appeared depicting 'The Iland called of olde Newfovnd land'. It was rather confusing. North faced downwards, so the southern part of the island was at the top of the page. Place-names were few, apart from a cluster on a peninsula that formed the south-eastern tip of Newfoundland. There, in large type, were the names 'Glamorgan' and 'Cambriola'. Settlements marked in smaller letters were 'Cardiffe', 'Carmarthi', 'Pembrok', 'Cardigan', 'Brechonia', and 'Golden Grove'. The map also included an inlet called 'Vaughan's Coue'. Less than a hundred years after the Act of Union which had absorbed Wales into England a new Wales seemed to be about to emerge on the far side of the Atlantic.

The mapmaker was named as 'Captaine Iohn Mason an industrious Gent: who spent seuen yeares in the Countrey'. Five years earlier, Mason's enthusiastic pamphlet 'A Briefe Discourse of the New-found-land' had been published in Edinburgh. It described the climate, flora and fauna of the island and its potential for settlement and development. Perhaps not surprisingly Mason's most purple prose was reserved for the fishery: '... of all, the most admirable is the Sea, so diuersified with seueral sorts of Fishes abounding therein, the consideration whereof is readie to swallow vp and drowne my senses not being able to comprehend or expresse the riches thereof.' Mason admitted that this might not appeal to the fastidious: '... peraduenture some squeaysie stomake will say, Fishing is a beastly trade & vnseeming a Gentleman.' However, he swept away such snobbishness with a well-chosen Latin tag, and went on to make a strong case for the superiority of his chosen colony over the settlements in Virginia and 'Birmooda'.

There was at least one Welshman who had no need to be converted by Mason's propaganda. William Vaughan came from one of the most important families in Carmarthenshire. He had been born in 1577, the second son of Walter Vaughan of Golden Grove. William was educated at Jesus College, Oxford. It may have been there that he acquired the Calvinism that was to shape his outlook on life. He completed his education by travelling through France and Italy, eventually reaching Vienna, where the university awarded him the degree of Doctor of Civil Law. The most dramatic event during these wanderings occurred on Christmas Day 1602. William was on a ship weathering rough seas off the French coast when he fell overboard. Having nearly drowned, he became convinced that God must have intervened to save him for some special purpose.

He was already the author of several books in English and Latin. These revealed his dedication to improving both agriculture and morals, particularly in Carmarthenshire. The impression given is of a serious, somewhat priggish, bookish young man with some very strongly held opinions. Marriage may have temporarily tamed his growing eccentricity. His wife Elizabeth was the daughter and heiress of David Llwyd ap Robert of Llangyndern. Through her William became the owner of Tor-y-coed.

Characteristically he changed its name to Terra Coed. He seems to have loved his wife dearly, a feeling that may have been deepened by the death of their only son.

In January 1608 there was a terrible storm. Terra Coed was struck by lightning. Elizabeth was killed but her husband escaped. William's cut-and-dried theology could only interpret this as a sign that God had once again shown his hand. The ensuing inner turmoil very nearly destroyed him. He was overwhelmed by a sense of guilt. This turned to paranoia as he became obsessed with the idea that rumours were circulating that he had in fact murdered his wife. The peculiar book that he published in 1611 entitled *The Spirit of Detraction conjured and convicted in Seven Circles* suggests a man at the end of his tether.

In the end his friends and relatives seem to have taken him in hand. The salvation which they offered took two forms. Firstly they found him a new wife with good financial prospects: one Anne Christmas from Colchester. Secondly they managed to interest him in the idea of establishing a 'Cambro-British' colony. In one of his early books William had lamented the decayed state of agriculture in Carmarthenshire. This new project offered the possibility of rescuing impoverished tenant farmers and labourers and their families from their misery. Gradually the idea of Cambriol began to take shape in William's mind, driving out the dark miseries that had plagued him.

William Vaughan was connected through his mother and step-mother with the greatest Welsh explorer of the day. Thomas Button came from near Cardiff. In 1612 he was put in charge of an expedition to find out what had happened to Henry Hudson, who had disappeared while trying to discover a north-west passage to Asia. Button's search involved spending the winter in the frozen wastes of Hudson's Bay. On his return he was knighted by James I. Button had named one of the inhospitable places that he had come across 'New Wales'. It may have been this that led William Vaughan to begin to dream of Cambriol. In 1616, the year in which he became High Sheriff of Carmarthenshire, William was assigned a tract of land in the Avalon peninsula by the Newfoundland Company.

Newfoundland seemed to be the obvious choice. God had placed it on the other side of the Atlantic from Wales, with only Ireland in the way. A ship setting out from Carmarthen, the busiest port in Wales at that time, could reach Newfoundland in a fortnight. Settlers could be transported out there for as little as ten shillings a head. The climate that they would find there would be very similar to that of West Wales. The area was not claimed by any other colonial power. The indigenous Beothuk Indians were only a few hundred strong and had retreated from the coastal area. Economic prospects were promising, particularly if fishing and farming were combined. As his plans began to take shape William Vaughan became convinced that Cambriol could not fail.

In 1617 a ship sailed from Carmarthen carrying the first party of Welsh colonists. Sickness prevented William from accompanying them. Leaderless and miserable the settlers spent their first winter at Aquafort on the Avalon Peninsula. It was there that Captain Richard Whitbourne found them when he arrived with a second Welsh group the following year. William Vaughan had appointed Whitbourne 'governor for life' of Cambriol. In return the Devon sea-captain and merchant helped to pay for the 1618 expedition. Whitbourne had first visited Newfoundland in 1579 and had been back to the island on many other occasions. In 1615 he had been officially appointed to look into disagreements about the Newfoundland fishery. It would have been hard to find a better-qualified candidate to turn William's dream into a reality – though Whitbourne's Englishness may have been partly responsible for his difficulties with the Welsh-speaking Carmarthenshire colonists.

The governor was scathing about what he found on his arrival. He described the settlers as 'idle persons ... which people had remained there a whole yeere, before I came neere, or knew any one of them; and in all which time they had not applied themselues to any commendable thing; no not so much as to make themselues an house to lodge in, but lay most shamefully in such cold and simple roomes all the winter, as the Fishermen had formerly built there for their necessary occasions, the yeere before those men arriued there.' Whitbourne's condemnation of the colonists as feckless squatters may be a little harsh. They seem to have been drawn from the most impoverished and desperate level of rural Carmarthenshire society. William Vaughan's enthusiasm had caught them up and dumped them on a strange shore on the far side of the Atlantic with little or no guidance as to what they should do next. That first winter in Cambriol must have been extremely bleak and depressing. They were no doubt relieved when the governor's ship eventually arrived.

Whitbourne realised that most of the would-be colonists were not cut out to be pioneers. He sent many of them back to Wales, including several of though who had crossed the Atlantic with him. A second ship had been meant to strengthen the settlement. Unfortunately it fell in with some former members of Sir Walter Raleigh's Guiana expedition. They had deserted and become pirates. The Cambriol ship was a tempting and easy prey for them. Its loss meant that the colony became desperately short of provisions. Whitbourne's solution was to move the little settlement down the coast to Renews (spelt 'Rhenus' by the pedantic William Vaughan).

The new location seemed to be an ideal centre for the colony. The inlet formed an excellent harbour. It was near some extremely rich fishing grounds and attracted large numbers of English fishing vessels every summer. There were crabs, lobsters and mussels in abundance and plenty of geese, ducks, and other wildfowl to feed the settlers during the winter months. However, by this time Whitbourne himself had begun to lose heart. He decided to return to England to look for a more reliable and stable partner than William Vaughan. Only six settlers were left to spend the winter in Cambriol. By 1619 they too had had enough and sailed for home.

If Gilliam T. Cell, the foremost modern expert on the settlement of Newfoundland, is to be believed, that was the end of Cambriol. Yet the Welsh colony continued to live on and develop and flourish in William Vaughan's fertile imagination. Ill-health and financial problems apparently prevented him for restarting the settlement and from visiting Newfoundland himself. Nevertheless, he continued to write about the island, and the belief grew (and is recorded in a Welsh history text book still used in schools) that he had in fact visited Cambriol in 1622. It was said that he devoted his time there to writing two literary works which he brought back to Wales with him in 1625. They were published under the pseudonym 'Orpheus Junior'. One was a Latin poem celebrating the marriage of Charles I to Henrietta Maria. The other,

The Golden Fleece, was a book about the commercial potential of the Newfoundland fishery, written in William's rambling, opaque style. It is sometimes claimed to be the first literary work in English composed in North America. Sadly this is untrue. Both publications included John Mason's map of Newfoundland with its many Welsh place-names.

By 1625 Cambriol was in fact nothing more than a dream. The Welsh settlements implied by the cluster of names on Mason's map existed only in William Vaughan's imagination. In 1628 he was knighted by Charles I, and there is a suggestion (dismissed by Cell) that he might have visited Newfoundland in that year. But even if he was indeed no more than an arm-chair enthusiast, Sir William's obsession with the island persisted and in 1630 he published a medical guide for would-be colonists entitled *The Newlanders Cure,* in which he wrote at length of the health-giving properties of turnips. It was his final attempt to encourage the revival of Cambriol. Shortly before his death in 1641 his last two books appeared. Both were religious works.

As historians have battled their way through Sir William Vaughan's vivid and sometimes confused imaginings to the kernel of truth at their heart, it has become clear that the first Welsh colony was a short-lived, rather desperate enterprise. The men and women who returned safely from it were no doubt relieved to be back home in Carmarthenshire. A winter spent shivering in stinking fish-gutting sheds on the rocky shores of Newfoundland must have made even the most hand-to-mouth existence in familiar surroundings seem attractive. Some of them later named their farms or smallholdings after the island that they had briefly visited. But for them the true 'new found land' was not Cambriol, but Wales. Having left it for a dream and then come home, they realised the true worth of the reality that they had so nearly turned their backs on for ever.

Singular shepherds:
some eccentric Welsh clergy
(Summer 2003)

My predecessors in the north Carmarthenshire hill parishes where I spent a large chunk of my ministry included several rather eccentric figures. Among them was an early nineteenth-century rector of Brechfa who owed his appointment entirely to his enthusiasm for playing football or *pêl ddu* ('black ball') as it was then called in rural Carmarthenshire.

Apparently a football match was scheduled to take place in Llangadog. Unfortunately one of the local players had not turned up and it looked as though the game would be cancelled, much to the annoyance of Squire Gwynne-Hughes of Tregib, who was an enthusiastic sportsman.

Among the spectators was Joshua Davies, the local curate. Like many junior clergy at the time he was pitifully poor and had a large family to feed. He was also a giant of a man who had obvious potential on the football field. Joshua remarked that he would be willing to fill the gap in the team, provided that it did not undermine his dignity as 'a man of cloth.' The squire overheard the curate's offer. In those pre-disestablishment days landowners very often controlled the appointments to Welsh parishes. Gwynne-Hughes suddenly remembered that he had a newly vacant parish in his gift. 'If you play in my team you can be the next rector of Brechfa,' he told the startled cleric. It was an offer that Joshua Davies couldn't refuse. He joined in the game and duly received his reward.

Joshua had ten children and Brechfa was not a wealthy parish. At first he supplemented his meagre income by conducting a small school. One of his pupils was William Thomas ('Gwilym Marles'), Dylan Thomas' great-uncle, who later achieved fame as a Welsh-language poet, Unitarian minister and radical political activist. William was not greatly impressed by his schoolmaster's educational attainments. He felt that Joshua should really have been a farmer. Squire Gwynne-Hughes must have been of the same mind. In the 1840s some of the Brechfa villagers became Mormons and emigrated to America. Several of the squire's farms became vacant. He offered one of them to the impoverished rector, who was thus able to end his days in a degree of comfort.

His move to Brechfa did not diminish Joshua's enthusiasm for football. Every Sunday morning after the church service the rector would gather the boys of the village for a riotous game of *pêl ddu* in Cae'r Palasau, the field behind the church. The strict Sabbath of Welsh Nonconformity was coming into fashion at the time, and the rector was sharply criticised by his chapel-going parishioners for such shameful behaviour.

Another of his little weaknesses was his enjoyment of a pint of beer in the evening. Teetotalism was also in vogue and there was pressure on Joshua to preach on the subject. He duly did so, remarking 'Don't do as I do, but do as I say.' When a Nonconformist acquaintance tried to persuade the ageing rector to take the pledge, Joshua refused to give in to him, saying 'I must have beer, but the people of Brechfa will be safe in heaven if they follow what I preach to them.'

Another rector of Brechfa had a very difficult start to his ministry there. Thomas Jones was inducted to the parish in January 1896 and found himself faced with an almost empty church. The root of the problem was the new rector's wife. It appears that she belonged to a family from a nearby village that had an ancient and bitter feud with some of the Brechfa folk. The church-people got together and decided to boycott the new incumbent's services in order to force him and his wife to move elsewhere.

On the road that leads from Brechfa to New Inn there was a little cottage known as the Lodge. The old couple who lived there were devout church members. One day, shortly before the new rector arrived, the husband went down to the village to do some shopping. He listened quietly while everyone around him talked excitedly about the lesson that they were going to teach the new rector and his wife. Then he returned home and repeated what he had heard. 'We shall be in church on Sunday,' his wife said firmly. When the day came the two old people walked down to Brechfa and sat in their usual pew. They were Thomas Jones' first congregation. Later in the week the new rector called at the Lodge. 'While there is a loaf on the Rectory table,' he said gratefully, 'half of it will be for you at the Lodge.'

As time went by Thomas Jones grew to be one of the best-loved and respected rectors that the parish had ever known. He grew a long white beard and wrote Welsh verses that were set to music by John Owen, the local composer. He also became increasingly absent-minded. On Sunday afternoons he would disappear down to the river to fish for salmon. There his sense of time would desert him, and Mrs Jones would have to dash over to the church and frantically ring the bell to remind him that he was supposed to be preaching at Evensong. When I went to Brechfa in the 1980s there were still several elderly church members who recalled *'yr hen Domos Jones'* with great affection. They also remembered being given toffees by Mrs Jones in Sunday School. The feud had eventually been set aside and she too had found acceptance in the parish.

Along the Cothi valley at Abergorlech the church was for many centuries a chapel-of-ease attached to the parish church of Llanybydder. There was a mountain between the two churches and because the eighteenth-century vicars of the parish received no payment for conducting services in this remote outpost they neglected it shamefully. The people of Abergorlech reacted by making their own arrangements. They invited the Methodist leader, Daniel Rowland, curate of Llangeitho, to come and celebrate Holy Communion for them. So many people turned out to hear Daniel that the tiny church could not hold them all. The result was that he held his service outside under an oak-tree that is still known as *'Derwen Daniel Rowland'*. Daniel Rowland persuaded the hymn-writer William Williams, who had recently been turned out of his curacy because of his Methodist leanings, to take unofficial charge of Abergorlech Church.

The vicar of the neighbouring parish of Llanfynydd was a man named Cornelius Copner. Under the terms of an endowment left by a godly Jacobite, Cornelius received £1 a year for preaching two Welsh sermons in Abergorlech on set dates in the year. Unfortunately both his preaching ability and his grasp of the Welsh language were somewhat deficient.

When the appointed time came round Cornelius saddled his horse and rode over to Abergorlech to deliver his sermon. To his surprise he discovered that, although there was a congregation inside the church, the door had been locked and bolted against him. The church people of Abergorlech held their own service, led by their unofficial curate, while the angry vicar of Llanfynydd hammered on the door, shouting to them to let him in. They ignored him and eventually Cornelius had to get back on his horse and return home, with his unpreached sermon still in his pocket and without the ten-shilling fee that he had hoped to receive for delivering it.

The row caused by this incident led the Bishop of St David's to find the small sum needed to employ an official curate for the chapel-of-ease. By the end of the nineteenth century Abergorlech was turned into a independent parish. Its two best-known twentieth-century vicars were respectively nicknamed '*Dafis Tew*' ('Fat Davies') and '*Dafis Tenau*' ('Thin Davies').

Dafis Tew was an enormous man who was greatly loved by his parishioners. He managed to scrape the money together to build a church hall during the depths of the economic depression between the two world wars. A suitably large picture of him still hangs on the wall of the building, looking down with a rotund and rather intimidating dignity on whist drives, children's parties and eisteddfodau.

His lean successor acquired a second nickname. One of the problems for any cleric on public occasions is how to express gratitude to everyone who has made some contribution. The danger is that a name will be inadvertently left out and an enormous row will follow. Dafis Tenau got round this problem with a single all-embracing sentence. Whatever the festivity or fund-raising event he would always stand up at the end and say solemnly (in English) 'I thank you one and all.' He would then sit down again. After a few years of this he merely had to stand up and there would be an immediate chorus of 'I thank you one and all' from every corner of the hall. In the end people stopped calling him Dafis Tenau and simply referred to him by the slogan that he had made his own.

At the end of the 1950s Brechfa and Abergorlech were united with the mountain parish of Llanfihangel Rhos-y-corn. It is said that every diocese in Wales has its 'punishment parish' and Llanfihangel Rhos-y-corn had the reputation of being the Siberia of St David's Diocese. It is said that anxious would-be clergy at St David's College, Lampeter, would regularly pray 'From Llanfihangel Rhos-y-corn save us, good Lord.'

Bishops normally forgot about Llanfihangel Rhos-y-corn and its incumbent. However the formidable Bishop John Owen decided to hold a confirmation there at the beginning of the twentieth century. Although the church had been standing for over six hundred years it is unlikely that any of his predecessors had bothered to visit it.

The then vicar had already been there for several years and both he and his wife were desperate to move to greener pastures. The confirmation service was followed by dinner at the vicarage. Throughout the meal the host and hostess attempted to persuade the bishop that he might them a more suitable and less remote parish. Bishop Owen did not respond. The next morning he asked the vicar to take him up to the crossroads at the top of the mountain. 'Where does that road go?' he asked. 'Llandeilo, my Lord.' 'And that one?' 'Lampeter, my Lord.' 'And the one over there?' 'Carmarthen, my Lord.' 'And that road goes to?' 'Llandysul, my Lord.' The bishop thought for a few moments and then pronounced his judgement. 'It's obviously very central. I think you'd better stay here.'

After the First World War the Forestry Commission bought up most of the farms in the parish and began to plant them with trees. The population shrank and the church authorities sometimes seemed to forget that Llanfihangel Rhos-y-corn and its vicar existed at all. One conscientious archdeacon suddenly realised that he never been to the parish or seen its incumbent. He decided to remedy this and set aside a day for an unannounced visit.

He was making his way up the mountain when he saw an old poacher coming towards him. The man wore a battered hat and a ragged jacket with a couple of rabbits stuffed in the pockets and was carrying a shotgun. It appeared that he had neither washed nor shaved for a considerable time. This disreputable figure was about to sidle past when the archdeacon stopped him. 'Excuse me, my man,' he asked, 'could you tell me the way to the vicarage?' 'Certainly, sir,' came the polite reply, 'It's just over there. I don't think you'll find the vicar in at present, but he should be at home in half and an hour or so.'

The archdeacon thanked the old ruffian and went on up the road to inspect the somewhat dilapidated church. Meanwhile the poacher climbed over a hedge with startling agility and raced across a field to the back door of the vicarage. When the archdeacon rang the doorbell some thirty minutes later he was met by a clean-shaven man with a well-scrubbed face wearing a clerical frock coat and collar. 'Mr Archdeacon,' this model clergyman exclaimed, 'What a wonderful surprise!'

George Noakes: a portrait

(April/May 2007)

We're told that no master is a hero to his valet. It's equally improbable for a vicar to be a hero to his curate – and yet there are exceptions that prove every rule. In 1979 I was appointed assistant curate of the parish of Aberystwyth in Ceredigion. Eric Roberts, the Bishop of St David's, had had great doubts about sending me there. I had been trained at the College of the Resurrection, Mirfield. It was a 'High Church' institution, run by an order of Anglican monks who were best known for their courageous opposition to apartheid in South Africa. The Rector of Aberystwyth and Archdeacon of Cardigan, the Venerable George Noakes, came from a 'Low Church' Evangelical background. Bishop Roberts was afraid that we might not get on with one another. He needn't have worried..

My 'training incumbent' (to use the ecclesiastical jargon) was a quite remarkable man. George Noakes came from Bwlch-llan in the depths of Ceredigion. His mother was from that area, and spoke beautiful Cardiganshire Welsh. His father was a descendant of the Flemings who had settled in South Pembrokeshire in medieval times. He had moved north to Bwlch-llan in search of work during the depression that hit rural Wales after the First World War, and had found a wife and a home there. The experience of being brought up on a bilingual hearth may explain why their son turned out to be such a sympathetic and effective teacher as he struggled to improve his curate's Welsh.

His *milltir sgwâr* of Ceredigion was also the source of George Noakes' deep commitment to ecumenism. As a child he was faithful in the parish church in Nantcwnlle, where his vocation to the ministry was nurtured by a devoted parish priest. However young George saw no contradiction in also regularly attending the Calvinistic Methodist (Welsh Presbyterian) chapel in Bwlch-llan. He had the same profoundly Christian disregard for denominational prejudices that characterised another great preacher from that corner of Wales: the eighteenth-century superstar Daniel Rowland of Llangeitho. When, as a curate, I used to go around Bronglais hospital to ask patients whether or not they would like to receive Holy Communion the following morning, my Rector's instructions were clear: "Offer Communion to everyone, whatever their denomination or background." The help and hope and comfort given by the Sacrament were what really mattered.

George Noakes was an enthusiastic sportsman from his schooldays in Tregaron onwards, until age and ill-health took their toll: a keen footballer, cricketer and fisherman. During the Second World War he was sent for R.A.F. training in Canada and ended up in one of the air-crews of Bomber Command, at a time when the life-expectancy of airmen involved in night-flying over Germany was agonisingly short. After graduating in philosophy from Aberystwyth University, he went on to Wycliffe Hall, Oxford, to train for ordination. He became Vicar of Eglwyswrw and then of Tregaron, after serving a curacy in Lampeter. Then came a move from the comparative peace of rural Ceredigion to Eglwys Dewi Sant, the Church in Wales' Welsh-language bastion in Cardiff. It was from there that he moved to Aberystwyth. His support in his work was Jean his gentle, self-effacing and extremely wise and perceptive wife.

Eglwyswyr (Welsh-speaking Anglicans), like their English-speaking counterparts, can easily become obsessed with ecclesiastical labelling. The 'churchmanship' of clergy is carefully delineated by the garb in which they celebrate the Eucharist: scarf and hood, surplice and stole or vestments. Religious jargon of various kinds is used as a shibboleth to distinguish between 'them' and 'us'. Cliques, pressure groups and 'party' organisations are formed of a type which St Paul, for one, would certainly have strongly condemned.

One of the wonderful things that I quickly discovered about my Rector in Aberystwyth was that he was totally uninterested in all that kind of nonsense. If he had to be put in a category it might, I suppose, have been that of a 'generous Evangelical' – though perhaps even more accurate would be a term borrowed from C.S. Lewis: a 'mere Christian'. At the heart of his ministry was a loving-kindness that reflected the loving-kindness of Jesus Christ himself.

The monks at Mirfield had taught me to pray (something that would later keep me going during many years of often very isolated rural ministry) and to conduct a service imaginatively without too much fussiness and with a decree of decorum – though they never succeeded in getting rid of what Rowan Williams (one of my contemporaries there) described as "Patrick's incurably Low Church walk". George Noakes completed my preparation for ministry in West Wales by showing me the importance of three other essentials: idiomatic Welsh, clear preaching and concern for people as individuals.

His patience with my initial mangling of the Welsh language was quite remarkable. We spoke together in Welsh almost from the beginning (once you have built up a relationship in one language it is very difficult to change to another one). This led to occasional moments of confusion. Once we had just left the Neuadd Fawr (Great Hall) on the university campus in Aberystwyth. The Rector had got into the driver's seat of his car, when he realised that he'd left his coat behind. "*Cer i nôl fy nghot o'r Neuadd, 'machgen i.*" I was heading back towards the building, when I suddenly realised that I hadn't the faintest idea what I was supposed to be looking for. Fortunately, once I was inside I spotted the coat and understanding dawned on me.

Preaching in Welsh is a very hazardous undertaking for any *dysgwr*. Anecdotes about appalling double-entendres inadvertently perpetrated by Welsh-learner preachers abound. George Noakes had bravely entrusted me with responsibility for St Mair, the Welsh language-church, sternly admonishing its members not to speak a word of English to me. Their patience and kindness was as great as his. But they couldn't help emitting the occasional giggle when one of my sermons included (for example) a word, dredged from the depths of the *Geiriadur Mawr*, which might have been totally innocuous in fourteenth-century Gwynedd but was utterly outrageous in twentieth-century Ceredigion.

George Noakes took me in hand. Every Friday night I would trot over to the Rectory with my laboriously prepared Welsh sermon, and he would carefully go through it with me. The result was a script covered with red ink. Nevertheless I was spared any more outbursts of unexpected laughter from my congregation. In the process my Rector also gave me some master classes in preaching. He was certainly the finest preacher of his generation in the Church in Wales, in Welsh, English and bilingually. Archbishop Michael Ramsey once said that good theology should combine simplicity and depth, and that combination was the essence of George Noakes' preaching.

As an enthusiastic young curate, fresh from the somewhat rarified atmosphere of a theological college, I needed to be shown how to translate high-flown ideas into accessible speech. I also had to be taught not to show off my supposed intellectual prowess. In one sermon I started holding forth about the early Christian theologian Irenaeus, a particular enthusiasm of mine. My Rector was not impressed (nor, coming to think of it, were the congregation). From then onwards I carefully avoided all such fancy references.

George Noakes was not only a great preacher – he was also an outstanding pastor. Whenever there's a pastoral crisis in the parish and I'm feeling flummoxed, my wife will still ask quietly, "What do you think Noakes would do?" He was especially kind to the old, the ill and the marginal: the sort of people who often get forgotten by the modern target-oriented church. He saw each person as being important. As the well-worn but worthwhile Welsh expression puts it: '*Roedd e wastad yr un peth i bawb*'.

One of the characters of the parish was a little old lady named Miss Benbow. She consumed a great deal of the clergy's time and could be a bit of a trial on occasions. George Noakes, however, always treated her with respect and thoughtfulness. Some years later, when he was Bishop, the Queen visited St David's, and there was a news clip of the two of them walking down to the Cathedral, chatting. "Look," my wife remarked "it's just like when he used to walk along talking to Miss Benbow." In George Noakes' eyes, as in God's, the Queen and the little old lady from Aberystwyth were of equal value.

Of course, he had his weaknesses. He would give up smoking for Lent – and then, after the seven o'clock Easter morning Eucharist in St Michael's, vanish swiftly out of the vestry door and round the back of St Michael's for a post-Lenten cigarette. He also had a deep dislike of dogs ('*fflipin' cŵn!*'), possibly based on bitter experience – some dogs go for clergy in much the same way that they go for postmen. When the pastoral visiting for the week was being allocated between us, he would make sure that I always got the houses where there were *cŵn*.

Being both Archdeacon of Cardigan and Rector of Aberystwyth was too great a burden, and so in 1980 Bishop Roberts moved him to a smaller parish. I felt bereft, though he still kept a kindly pastoral eye on my progress, and not long afterwards we were both among a party of pilgrims from the Aberystwyth area that visited the Holy Land. The memory that lingers is of George Noakes standing on a hill in Galilee, looking around him with a huge smile, and exclaiming "*Mae hwn yn gymwys yr un peth â Sir Aberteifi!*" ("This is exactly like Cardiganshire!") Strangely enough, it was.

I moved on to St Peter's, Carmarthen, for a second curacy. In 1981 Archdeacon George Noakes was elected Bishop of St David's. He moved to Llys Esgob, the Bishop's house at Abergwili outside Carmarthen. One afternoon I returned from parish visiting to be greeted by my wife. "The Bishop's just called," she said excitedly, "and what's more, he hasn't changed a bit!"

Being elevated to the purple can do terrible things to ordinary, decent, hard-working priests. Some become autocratic, others become paranoid or pompous. George Noakes had none of these failings. Bishops have to wear some extremely peculiar clothes. It is quite difficult not to look silly in a mitre – and at the time that George Noakes was consecrated the comedian Dave Allen was famous for his hilarious bishop impressions. Bishop George always kept a mental picture of Dave Allen in mind, and it saved him from any excesses of episcopal foolishness. As one of my churchwardens up in the hills once remarked: "*Rwy'n hoff o Noakes – mae e'n ddyn ishel iawn.*" ("I'm fond of Noakes – he's a very humble man.").

During his enthronement at St David's Cathedral, Bishop George made his own special addition to the liturgy. As he moved towards the West Door after his consecration, he arranged for a chorister to call out the words addressed by the Greeks to Philip: "Sir, we wish to see Jesus." The desire to make Jesus known to the people of his diocese and later of the whole of Wales became the touchstone of George Noakes' work as Bishop of St David's and Archbishop of Wales. It was a task that he assumed with characteristic conscientiousness.

Sadly, that conscientiousness proved his undoing. His inability to cut down on a crushing workload undermined his health and he was eventually forced to retire. Yet he remains an inspiration, not just for those who visit him in his retirement, but to everyone whom he has touched throughout his ministry. Certainly his example, kindness and friendship have had a lasting impact on my own life. He may well be the most undervalued of twentieth-century Welsh spiritual leaders, but I suspect that that doesn't bother him very much. What matters more to him are all those people whom he did indeed teach 'to see Jesus'. It is a privilege to be among them.

The land under the waves

(Autumn 1999)

At Wallog, between Borth and Aberystwyth, a narrow spit of shingle, gravel and large stones stretches out into Cardigan Bay. It is known as *Sarn Cynfelyn* (Cynfelyn's causeway) after a sixth-century saint who lived not far away. Several miles out to sea a channel separates the submerged spit from the shoals known as *Cynfelyn Patches*, a part of which was once occasionally visible above the water. One early nineteenth-century maps *Sarn Cynfelyn* is shown as a narrow sandbank reaching all the way to these rocks, which are various named as *Caernyddno, Caernyddw* or *Caer Wyddno*.

Gwyddno was the legendary king of the lost territory of Cantre'r Gwaelod (the bottom hundred). In the minds of those who drew the maps and those who looked at them *Sarn Cynfelyn* had once been the road to a Welsh Atlantis, and the insignificant cluster of offshore rocks was all that remained of the fortress of the unfortunate ruler of a kingdom submerged for ever as the waters surged across Cardigan Bay. Drowned cities exercise an extraordinary pull on the human imagination. The story of *Cantre'r Gwaelod* is no exception.

The core of the legend is a mysterious group of *englynion* in the Black Book of Carmarthen, the thirteenth-century manuscript that is the earliest surviving substantial collection of Welsh poetry. They are addressed to a man named Seithennin and speak of the way in which the sea has covered a place called *Maes Gwyddno*. The poems were probably part of a now lost prose saga describing the inundation. The storyteller would have used them to provide dramatic emphasis as the tale unfolded.

In the first stanza the poet calls on Seithennin to get up and come and look at the raging of the sea that has drowned *Maes Gwyddno*. The next two verses curse a maiden who had apparently been responsible for unleashing the waters. It appears that she had acted as the servant of the wild and desolate sea, unstopping the spring from which it had gushed forth. There is a hint that she may have done this because she was sorrowing for someone killed in battle.

The maiden's name is given us in the next five *englynion*. She is called Mererid. She stands on the battlements wailing, pleading with God to forgive her for the destruction that she has caused. The poet has no sympathy for her – only anger. He regards her actions as having been caused by '*traha*', the arrogant pride which is the Welsh equivalent of hubris in the Greek tragedy. *Traha* leads to disaster. At one point Mererid is described as being on the back of a beautiful chestnut horse, perhaps being rescued from the disaster. In the end the poet gets fed up with her screeching and leaves his room to escape from it.

The final verse returns to 'proud Seithennin'. It is an *englyn* which has already appeared earlier in the Black Book of Carmarthen in a collection of stanzas describing where the graves of various heroes and important figures can be found. We are told that Seithennin was 'a noble warrior' and that his grave is between *Caer Cenedir* and the sea shore.

The Black Book verses certainly give us the skeleton of a story. It might be reconstructed as follows. There was once a land called *Maes Gwyddno* ruled by a warrior king named Seithennin. It was a low-lying area and the sea was a constant threat. However, the land was safe, provided a particular stone was not moved. This stone might have been the cover over a spring or well, or it may have been part of the sea wall.

Among Seithennin's servants was a girl named Mererid. She was in love with one of Seithennin's soldiers. The king went to war and Mererid's boyfriend was killed in the fighting. In a fit of rage and anguish the young woman decided to be revenged on the king whose warmongering had deprived her of the person she loved best. Mererid moved the one stone that should never be moved. Water gushed forth and soon the furious sea had overwhelmed *Maes Gwyddno*.

Mererid quickly realised the terrible mistake that she had made. She stood on the battlements above the surging sea and screamed at God, asking him to forgive her, and pleading with him to undo and set right the terrible destruction that she had unleashed on her land. As she escaped on horseback from the horror she continued to lament. The storyteller ended his tale with exact directions as to where Seithennin's grave could be found – just in case anyone had any doubts about the king's existence or the truth of what they had just heard.

A good story changes shape as it passes from mouth to mouth. Some elements are developed or embroidered, others are left out. New characters may appear, original characters may start behaving in a different way. What matters is whether the story is a tale worth telling and re-telling. The factual truth of its contents is neither here nor there, though a story worth repeating often touches on fundamental truths about the way people are: what they hope for, and what they fear.

Another thirteenth-century Welsh manuscript describes Seithennin as king of *Maes Gwyddno*, and tells us that his lands were drowned by the sea. By the fifteenth century, however, Gwyddno himself has become a character in the story, and his lament for his lost land is as powerful as that of the hapless Mererid. The poet Guto'r Glyn, casting around for a suitable comparison to convey the depths of his sorrow at the death of one of his patrons, the abbot of Strata Florida, says it is like 'the lament of Gwyddno Garanhir, across whose land God turned the sea'.

Gwyddno becomes the king, supplanting Seithennin. Place-names along the shores of Cardigan Bay begin to cement his relation with the drowned lands. The rocks of *Caer Wyddno* (Gwyddno's fortress) have been mentioned, while the full name of the seaside town of Borth, north of Aberystwyth, is said to be *Porth Wyddno yng Ngheredigion*. A proverb from that part of Wales is almost identical to Guto'r Glyn's couplet, referring to 'the sigh of Gwyddno Garanhir when the wave turned across his land'. Gwyddno also becomes linked to the traditions surrounding the legendary shape-changing poet Taliesin. Elffin, Gwyddno's son, comes across the infant poet in his father's *'gored'* (fish weir) 'on the beach between Dyfi and Aberystwyth near his own castle'. The castle was presumably *Caer Gwyddno*, that mysterious rocky shoal beyond the end of *Sarn Cynfelyn*.

Once Gwyddno had become king a new rôle had to be found for Seithennin. Help was provided by the existence of another ridge of pebbles stretching out beneath

Cardigan Bay. Sarn Badrig (Patrick's causeway) lies to the north of the Barmouth Estuary. A seventeenth-century Merionethshire antiquary decided that it must be the remains of a large stone wall that had once defended the lands of Gwyddno from the sea. In the mid-eighteenth century Lewis Morris suggested that *Cantre'r Gwaelod* was protected by dams and floodgates and that the disaster had happened because someone got drunk and left the floodgates open. The inclusion of drunkenness in the story seems to have stemmed from a misunderstanding about a word in the Black Book of Carmarthen poems. *'Gwineu'* means 'bay' or 'chestnut' and refers to the colour of Mererid's horse. Morris mistranslated it as 'wines' – and the idea of a wild and disastrous booze-up in Cantre'r Gwaelod was born.

It is hardly surprising that one of Wales' most imaginative storytellers, the poet, literary forger and opium addict Iolo Morganwg, seized on this new element in the tale when he was manufacturing some supposedly medieval triads (those lists of three which early Welsh storytellers leant by heart to help them remember their huge repertoire of stories). Iolo conjured up a triad about the 'Three Out-and-out Drunkards of the Island of Britain'. Number three was 'Seithennin the Drunken son of Seithyn Saidi, king of Dyfed, who when drunk released the sea over Cantre'r Gwaelod, until all the houses and land that were there were lost, where before there were sixteen cities, the best of all the towns and cities of Wales ... *Cantre'r Gwaelod* was the wealth of Gwyddno Garanhir, king of Ceredigion; and that was in the time of Emrys Wledig (Ambrosius Aurelianus); and the people who escaped from that deluge settled in Ardudwy, and the land of Arfon, and the Snowdon mountains, and other places that were uninhabited before that.'

Mererid the proud maiden had disappeared from the story and responsibility for the tragedy shifted to Seithennin, now demoted to the post of inebriated keeper of the floodgates. Other minds (not all of them as gifted as Iolo Morganwg) began to create their own versions of the legend. A certain T. Jeffrey Llewelyn Prichard published a lengthy poem entitled 'The Land beneath the Sea or Cantrev y Gwaelod' in 1826. Prichard thought that it was far too unpoetic to portray Seithennin as a drunk. Instead he turned him into a jealous lover. Rona, one of the beauties of Cantre'r Gwaelod, had spurned Seithennin in favour of Elffin, Gwyddno's son. In revenge Seithennin imported a band of well-paid villains who undermined the sea wall. At the next story Gwyddno's kingdom was overwhelmed.

A much greater writer, Thomas Love Peacock, used the Cantre'r Gwaelod legend as the basis for his novel *The Misfortunes of Elphin*, which appeared three years after Prichard's lamentable effort. Peacock turns Seithennin back into a toper, whose neglect of his duties as 'Lord High Keeper of the Royal Embankment' leads to the flooding of Gwyddno's land. A magazine story of 1859 added yet another slant to the story: the idea that visitors to the Aberdyfi area might sometimes hear the distant ringing of the bells of the drowned churches of *Cantre'r Gwaelod*.

The legend continues to attract interpreters. One fine recent version is by the Cardiganshire writer T. Llew Jones in his collection of folktales *Lleuad yn Olau*. Gwyddno Garan Hir is king of *Cantre'r Gwaelod*. He has appointed Prince Seithennin as guardian of the walls. One night the king holds a great feast to celebrate his daughter's birthday. Seithennin and his men go to the feast leaving only two young watchers on the walls. One of them, Gwyn ap Llywarch, a poor nobleman's son, is secretly in love with Mererid, Gwyddno's daughter. There is a terrible storm. Gwyn's companion runs to the feast to rouse Seithennin and his assistants, but they are too drunk to do anything. The sea wall caves in. Gwyn grabs a horse from the stables and rescues Mererid, taking her to the safety of Aberarth, above Cardigan Bay. The two of them weep for their land that has vanished beneath the waves. Then they set off together to make a new home in the hills. In his retelling of the legend T. Llew Jones succeeds in recovering some elements from the early poems that had been ignored by other recent storytellers.

Is there really a drowned land beneath Cardigan Bay? The geologist F. J. North, author of *Sunken Cities*, the most detailed study of the background to the tradition, dismisses the idea of a major inundation. He does, however, conclude that 'sudden flooding on a limited scale ... could have taken place here and there along the shores of a Cardigan Bay known to human beings'. His suggestion is that 'stories of the destruction of a few homesteads gradually grew into a legend telling of the sudden loss of a region ...' Yet those mysterious verses in the Black Book of Carmarthen still catch the imagination with their echoes of a devastating tragedy – while even the most prosaic stroller along the sands at Aberdyfi is tempted to listen out for the sound of the bells of *Cantre'r Gwaelod*.

Dafydd in love:
a poet and his women

(Winter 1997)

It was the usual Sunday Mass in the ancient church of Llanbadarn Fawr, near Aberystwyth. The congregation were there for a mixture of reasons. Some had come to pray, others to hear the latest gossip or to show off their clothes. One, at least, was there to make an impression on a pretty girl:

> There was never a Sunday in Llanbadarn
> (Others will back me up on this)
> When I wasn't looking at a fair girl
> With my back towards God's presence.

The young poet stared longingly over the plumes of his hat at the object of his desire. One of her friends noticed and remarked:

> "That pale lad with a girlish face
> And his sister's hair on his head
> Squints like an adulterer:
> He's used to misbehaving."

To which his beloved enchantress replied:

> "Is that what he's got in mind?
> He'll get no answer while the world lasts;
> Let him go to the devil, the silly fool!"

At which the rejected lover grimly contemplated becoming a hermit.

The amorous poet was the fourteenth-century writer Dafydd ap Gwilym. He had been born at Bro Gynin, a few miles from Llanbadarn. His poetry celebrates the beauty of that area and the charms of its women. Occasionally he wandered further afield. One of his most famous poems describes an amatory adventure in a city inn which (predictably) ended in disaster.

A beautiful serving wench with black eyebrows had attracted Dafydd's attention. He managed to get her to sit next to him on the bench and then, after some skilful chatting-up, arranged to meet her when everyone else had gone to bed. When the guests were all safely snoring Dafydd set out to find her. Unfortunately he tripped over a stool in the dark, banging his head on a table. The table then collapsed, sending a noisy brass saucepan clattering to the floor. The dogs began to bark and the row woke up three English pedlars. They began to shout that a Welsh thief was on the loose and a search was started. Dafydd hid, praying hard. Somehow he managed to find his way back to his own lonely bed.

He had better success with Elen Nordd (or North), the money-loving, men-chasing wife of one of the prominent citizens of the little Anglicized borough of Aberystwyth. Robin Nordd was a bald English wool merchant, while Elen herself spoke Welsh with a marked English accent. Dafydd shows little real affection for her in the only poem in which she gets a mention. He was, however, delighted to cuckold her unattractive husband in exchange for a load of top quality woollen stockings.

The two women who really captured Dafydd's affection were Morfudd and Dyddgu. At one time it was thought that they were both fictional characters, dreamed up by the poet to reflect two different ideals of womanhood. Morfudd is fair-haired. Her affair with Dafydd is consummated, but she is fickle and faithless and ends up marrying a man whom the poet loathes. Dyddgu is dark, aloof and well-bred – a descendant of the royal princes of Deheubarth. In the end Dafydd is forced to admit that his love for her will never be returned. Research has revealed that the two women did indeed exist. Morfudd's husband *Y Bwa Bach* ('the little hunchback') appears to have lived within a mile of Dafydd's birthplace at Bro Gynin. Dyddgu is now thought to have been the daughter of an uchelwr (one of the Welsh gentry) from Tywyn.

Morfudd inspired some of Dafydd's most beautiful poetry. In 'Stolen Love' he remembers a secret meeting with her in one of his favourite settings:

> It was lovely meeting together,
> Hiding together in the woods,
> Wandering together along the seashore,
> Staying together at the edge of the trees,
> Happily planting birches together,
> Together plaiting beautiful greenery,
> Discussing love together with a slender girl,
> Looking together at faraway fields.
> Walking together through a wood with her love
> Is a blameless activity for a girl,
> Dignified, smiling together,
> Laughing together and kissing,
> Falling down together near the grove,
> Avoiding people together, complaining together,
> Gently being together, drinking mead together,
> Guiding love together, lying together,
> Together catching hold of secret love,
> Faithful – there's no more to be said.

Dafydd would choose 'love messengers' to send to Morfudd, making them the theme of his poems to her. A seagull and a thrush carried his love to her – as did the wind itself:

> I was to be pitied when I seriously fell
> For Morfudd my matchless love -
> A girl who made me an exile.

Run through the air to her father's house.
Knock on the door, make her answer
My message before dawn.
Try to reach her if you can,
And tell her all my worries.
Come down from the majestic universe
And tell my generous, lively love:
I am her faithful love-servant
While I live in this world.
My life is wretched without her
If it's true that she's faithful.
Go up, and if you see a fair-faced girl,
Go down, sky's friend.
Go to a golden-haired maiden -
Then, sky's companion, come home safely.

The freshness of Dafydd's poems to Morfudd is startling. He combines the technical skills of the old princely court poetry (the craft of alliteration, internal rhyme and 'tongue music' which sadly gets lost in translation) with the flexibility and humour of the more down-to-earth folk poets. But he also draws on the type of lyrical love poetry developed by the Provençal troubadours which had become fashionable throughout Europe. Dafydd was the product of a multilingual culture. In addition to his extraordinary command of his native Welsh he also seems to have been at least partially fluent in English, French and Latin. He might well be described as the first Welsh European. He draws on these rich resources to portray a love affair that is complex and sometimes extremely painful.

One of Dafydd's most remarkable poems, 'Morfudd like the Sun', brilliantly expresses the tension (of which he is only too aware) between the ideal he has created of the woman he is loves and the reality of her fickle nature:

She's deceitful and a trickster,
Worse than anything, yet she's my love.
Sometimes my fair girl appears
In church and court.....
At other times bright shining Morfudd sets
Like a fair fringed sun:
Nurse of fine weather's princedom.
Her wise work deserves praise,
May's merchant woman, generous with light.
Bright Morfudd is long-expected:
A lovely mirror to the Virgin Mary's splendour.

It has been suggested that one particularly bitter poem may have been written after

Morfudd's marriage. In 'Love's Husbandry' Dafydd uses the rhythm of medieval rural life to reflect the depth of his feeling of rejection and betrayal:

> I ploughed the land in winter
> And was paid with lovesickness;
> Between the dead month's time
> And Morfudd's love (the hidden infection grew)
> The happy, fearless, serious breast was ploughed
> As a deep blow cut a furrow,
> While a wise and perfect plough
> Prepared the other breast.
> The ploughshare's in my heart
> And love's coulter is above the slopes.
> And in the right breast (a quick wound),
> Sowing and levelling in a flood of passion.
> After three months (well-chosen thought),
> In springtime (peirced by sleeplessness' deceit)
> Worry took root in me....

The anguish continued. His love grew and seemed likely to bring forth an abundant crop, that would need plenty of reapers. And then disaster struck:

> The wind turned (a far-reaching blow)
> From the south of the heart split in two
> And darkened two stars of love
> In my head (fury's my mistress)
> My eyes were open gates for angry tears
> To flow through, passion's swimmers;
> They looked (inflamed with tears)
> At Morfudd, the splendid, gentle girl...
>
> An angry storm from the west
> Damages stubble (an armful of anguish);
> And heavy, sad and ceaseless rain comes
> From the eastern sky on my two cheeks.
> Large tears because my beautiful one
> (A ruined crop) stops my eyes from sleeping.

This gloomy response to Morfudd's faithlessness didn't prevent Dafydd from trying to rekindle their past love. Her hunch-backed husband, *Y Bwa Bach,* acquires another nickname: *Eiddig* – 'the jealous one'. One of Dafydd's disaster poems, 'Eiddig's Three Porters', describes an attempt (real or imaginary) to find a way into Morfudd's house so that he can see her again. The raid is thwarted. A savage dog, a squeaky door and Eiddig's maid ('a witch' according to the poet) are the 'three porters' that warn

Morfudd's husband that there is an intruder. Dafydd's expedition is frustrated, and he has to make do with whispering sweet nothings through the thick stone wall:

> Angrily I retreated back
> To the door, with the stinking dog after me.
> With a shiver of terror
> I ran without delay along the wall
> Around the shining, splendid court
> To await my beautiful gem.
> I shot through the wall (painful burden)
> Arrows of love towards the slim girl.
> She, from her lovely, shining breast
> Shot her love as a message to me.
> I enjoyed (love doesn't disappoint me)
> Having only a stone wall between me and the slender girl.
> I complained, I told her my anger,
> As I had to, outside Eiddig's door.

His problems with Morfudd's husband finally led Dafydd to reject her as the object of his poetry and his passion. Instead he transferred his attention to the beautiful but hopelessly unattainable Dyddgu. Even though he would never succeed in luring her to the bed of leaves in the birch grove where he and Morfudd had once enjoyed themselves, Dafydd could at least put Dyddgu on a pedestal and pour out his love for this 'girl with dark and shining eyes' from a polite and respectful distance. In 'Morfudd and Dyddgu' he charts the change in his affections. Dyddgu is the image of perfection:

> Poor me (it's pitiful)
> That I never knew,
> Before I came to the marrying age,
> What it was to love a girl who was gentle, pretty, slender, good,
> Greatly gifted, faithful, wise,
> Skilled at playing, beloved, polite,
> Well-spoken like a landowner,
> Well-bred, with proper passions, truthful,
> Shapely, unfussy, full
> Of talents and of knowledge,
> As lovely and fair as lively Indeg,
> Virgin land (I'm a young ox),
>
> A love you can depend on,
> A golden rod with a shining forehead
> (Deserving the widest praise)
> Is Dyddgu, with her dark, smooth eyebrows.

Poor Morfudd pales into insignifance beside this paragon. The frustration which has built up in Dafydd bursts out in a denunciation of his erstwhile lover and her husband, which shows that the three of them had come to resemble characters in a Brian Rix farce:

> Morfudd's not like that -
> She's like this (the red-hot ember!)
> Loving those who tell her off,
> A stubborn, very wearisome girl,
> Respected owner of a house
> And husband, a very pretty girl.

> It's not less frequently that I've fled
> At midnight, because of her,
> From her husband and her large, windowed house,
> Than in the day (I'm good at jumping!);
> Leaving her tough husband, with unwise words,
> Clapping his hands together.
> He always shouts (the lusty man)
> And yells because his children's mother has been stolen.

Dafydd ends the poem by saying that of the two women he chooses Dyddgu, 'if she is to be had.'

His final description of Morfudd comes in a poem about her old age. Her beauty has vanished: 'The Creator has made her ugly.' The transformation is chilling, particularly when one remembers what she once had been like:

> She was formed enchantingly,
> A sorceress, a lovely thief.
> Now she's bent like the beam of an Irish mangonel,
> A cold, abandoned summer house – she who was fair.

Dafydd ap Gwilym is a poet of love and springtime. He represents that rash, irresponsible and yet charmingly attractive side of the Welsh character which is in constant conflict with the Puritanical guilt that is the other side of our nature (the Irish and the Scots have the same problem). In one of his poems Dafydd meets a grey friar who sharply condemns both his womanizing and his versifying. The poet's response is a plea for beauty and cheerfulness which may stand as his final testament:

> I answered the Brother
> For every word he said:
> 'God is not so cruel
> As old men say.

God won't let a gentle man's soul be lost
Because he loves a woman or a maiden.
Three things are loved throughout the world:
A woman, fair weather and health.

A girl is the fairest flower
In Heaven except God himself.
Every man in every nation
Was born of a woman except three.
And so it isn't strange at all
That girls and women are loved.
Joy comes from Heaven
And every sadness comes from Hell.

Fighting for Christmas:
Matthew Owen of Llangar, carol writer and patriot

(December2006/January 2007)

One ancient Welsh Christmas custom is the singing of *'carolau dan bared'* – carols sung from house to house. The singers would, of course, hope to receive a cheerful welcome from the householders: a chance to come in and warm themselves by the fire, with the hope of a drink or two to fortify them for the rest of their journey. As a part of that venerable tradition, during my years as a country priest in the hills and forests of north Carmarthenshire, I used to join up with a few courageous souls, tramping the lanes around the hamlet of Gwernogle, at the foot of Mynydd Llanfihangel Rhos-y-corn.

It was always extremely dark and either pouring with rain or bitterly cold. The quality of our singing left much to be desired, but our enthusiasm was boundless. One incentive was the knowledge that the welcome at our last two ports of call would be kind and generous. At London House (whose name betrayed the fact that it had once been a village shop) Tom and Yvonne Thomas would revive our spirits with a glass or two of invigorating elderflower wine. The journey's end would be the farm kitchen at Pant-y-coubal, where Idris Evans would produce a bottle of sherry to coax a final effort from our strained and battered vocal chords.

Before dawn on Christmas morning, in the little church of St Teilo, Brechfa, I would find myself sharing in another Welsh carolling custom. *Plygain* comes from the Latin for the crowing of the cockerel, and refers to the early hour at which the service was held (in our case at six o'clock in the morning). It has its origins in the medieval Welsh church. In some places it derived from the early morning mattins of Christmas Day, and thus became a shortened morning prayer with the appropriate Bible readings, followed by carol-singing. In other churches it seems to have been linked more closely with one or other of the first two masses of Christmas: the midnight Mass of the Angels or the early morning Mass of the Shepherds.

Our Brechfa *Plygain* derived from the latter, which was particularly appropriate as a great many of those present at the service were sheep farmers and their families. It would begin by candlelight, with a carol sung unaccompanied by a group of men, most of whom were forestry workers or young farmers. The atmosphere was unforgettable: for a few minutes Brechfa became Bethlehem, and the small church was transformed into the stable behind the inn, where the shepherds came to pay homage to the new-born baby: *'Duw yn y byd fel dyn bach'* ('God in the world as a tiny child'), as one of our local poets described him.

There was a brief period in Welsh history when singing carols either in church or around the houses was outlawed. On December 24th 1652 an edict was published by Parliament: 'That no observation shall be had of the five and twentieth day of December, commonly called Christmas Day; nor any solemnity used or exercised in churches upon that day in respect thereof.'

The ban was greeted with horror in Wales. An anonymous poet attacked the new rulers of the church for being 'opposed to the revered Holy Days…casting down Christmas from the way it used to be.' The devout Breconshire layman Henry Vaughan, one of the greatest Welsh writers in the English language in any age, compared the government's actions to those of a pagan Roman emperor. For most ordinary Welsh people the prohibition of Christmas and the customs associated with it were yet another example of English tyranny. A backlash was inevitable.

Matthew Owen of Llangar, a young Welsh-language poet from Edeirnion, spearheaded the reaction. He was living in Oxford in the 1650s and some sources say that he might have gone there as a student, though apparently he never took a degree. An autobiographical reference in one of his poems suggests that he was actually a glover (or a glover's apprentice) by trade. In 1656 he composed two carols which he sent home to Wales.

The first was intended to be sung by a party of carollers going from house to house. It begins innocently enough, following a traditional pattern. Owen addresses the 'famously generous' family of the house that is being visited, who are 'keeping the holy day according to virtuous custom' and are 'used to enjoying sweet music, praising Christmas with a contented gentle tune.' He calls on them to welcome the carollers, and vividly expresses the singers' feelings:

> We're made miserable by cold: until we see a blazing fire
> We'll never be able to sing properly.
> And our musician is the same: outside, with hoarfrost on his nails,
> He won't be able to manage a sweet tune.

And then the satire starts to creep in. People should voluntarily open their doors to the carollers who have come 'cheerfully and carefully through difficult weather…to commemorate lovingly the blessed and comforting festival.' But if they refuse, Matthew Owen's singers have a secret weapon up their sleeve:

> We have an order from the Lord Protector
> To make everyone open the door – what lazy person won't get up?
> It was made in Oxford, it was printed in London,
> And sent from there to Corwen.

> And we first received it between Wrexham and Bala:
> A warrant to keep this festival in spite of every mad ruffian.
> If anyone won't open up, wherever we sing tonight,
> We'll insist on fining him a verse.

Owen ridicules Lord Protector Cromwell by using a bogus proclamation to promote Christmas rather than to suppress it. In the process the late night 'knock on the door' that is so terrifying for opposition supporters under any dictatorial regime, is subverted and supplanted by a cheerfully festive 'knock on the door' that brings music, enjoyment and celebration.

The poet ends his carol with an expression of his own sincere faith in '*yr Oen gwrol*' ('the brave Lamb'):

> His pure birth and his extreme courage,
> And his praise and his death are known to all.
> If we believe in them, through pure uncorrupted faith,
> We shall be in holy Jesus' company for ever and ever.

The tendency to stereotype the conflicts of mid-seventeenth century Wales as being between religious and irreligious groupings is misleading. Both Puritans and anti-Puritans (like Matthew Owen) were people with deeply held beliefs. Cromwell's Welsh supporters wished to ban Christmas, seeing it as a superstitious festival that had no place in a 'purified' version of Christianity. Henry Vaughan spoke for their opponents in describing the abolition of Christmas as an attempt 'to extinguish the memory of [Christ's] Incarnation.'

Matthew Owen was determined that Cromwell and his sympathisers should not succeed. As well as his carol for singing around the houses, with its satiric edge, he also composed an epic fifty-two verse poem which he described as 'A Chronicle *Plygain* Carol, expressing the Birth and Suffering of JESUS, and the history of the Welsh from the beginning.' Traditional *Plygain* carols are usually fairly lengthy and didactic in tone, tending to include the whole history of salvation as well as the Christmas story. Owen's *Plygain* carol was written not only to emphasize the doctrinal significance of Christmas, but also to underline the importance of the festival in Welsh Christian tradition. The patriotic exile composed this substantial work to encourage any brave Welshmen and women who were prepared to defy Cromwell's decree and make their way to church before dawn on Christmas day to celebrate the birth of their Saviour.

The lengthy carol intertwines Biblical references and a version of Welsh origins that owes much to the creative imagination of Geoffrey of Monmouth. It begins in Eden and continues with Noah and the Deluge. Once the floodwaters have subsided Noah's son Japheth goes to Natalia (Anatolia) and founds the great city of Troya (Troy). The Trojans become too proud and the Greeks burn the city, but Eneas escapes. His descendant, Brutus, lands on the Isle of Wight in 1108 BC, defeats the local giants and takes over the country, building cities and splendid palaces.

He and his fellow Britons are still pagans, living 'in great darkness... deserving the wrath of the faultless God of Heaven and grievous damnation.' Fortunately Owen's God has looked more kindly on a nation over in '*Gorllewin, isel Assia*' ('low West Asia'). Moses and the prophets had told its inhabitants about the future birth of 'a King and a redeemer.' Gabriel's visit to Mary and the birth of Jesus are described, while the account of the angels and the shepherds echoes the *Plygain* service itself:

> At the beginning of the happy cheerful *Plygain*
> A host of Holy Angels came;
> Openly praising God together,
> In a place where there were poor shepherds.

> They told of the birth of the true Gracious Son,
> As the world's manifest Saviour;
> And the shepherds went to the town
> To look for him, cheerfully.
>
> They found the Son of the Triune God
> In Bethlehem, wrapped in clothing.
> The Holy One was in the manger,
> They directed their praise to him.

Owen swiftly moves through the story of Christ's life, death, crucifixion and resurrection. He then returns to the subject of the secret disciple who had taken Jesus' body down from the cross:

> And he who put him in the tomb,
> Through pure and faithful kindness,
> Was called gentle Joseph
> From the good land of Arimathea.
>
> Before long this Joseph came
> To walk through fertile Britain,
> Spreading the praiseworthy Gospel
> Among the skilfully built temples and fortresses.

Now the poet is back in the familiar comforting waters of Geoffrey of Monmouth's mythology, which he uses to combine his patriotism and his religious beliefs. He tells how the first king anywhere to become a Christian was Lucius, 'chief ruler of Britain' (and therefore an ancestor of the Welsh), and goes on to speak of the cheerfulness with which 'our forefathers' adopted Christianity. Modern historians may argue that the Emperor Constantine's mother was a Romanian innkeeper's daughter, but Owen, following a deep-rooted medieval Welsh tradition, insists that she was a '*Brytanes*', who strengthened the link between the Holy Land and Wales by finding Christ's Cross and bringing it back to her homeland.

According to the *Geiriadur Prifysgol Cymru*, the Welsh word *Nadolig* (Christmas) comes from the colloquial Latin *Natalicia*. Matthew Owen, however, suggests that the name of the festival was given to the Welsh by Jesus himself. He also stresses the respect in which the Twelve Days of Christmas were held by 'the powerful King Arthur and the fine Britons after him...'

For the exiled carol writer from Llangar, Christmas is an essential part of the Welsh spiritual tradition. He notes that the attack on the Holy Days is something very recent, and suggests that the best way to fight back is by celebrating Christmas with more enthusiasm than ever:

But the sects of this age arose,
Denying the happy Holy Days.
The more that they blaspheme against Christmas,
The more we shall praise it.

Let us praise our God by respecting the Day
With holy faith and love;
Hoping we'll have, on Judgement Day,
Christ as our strong Saviour.

Matthew Owen sent his *Plygain* carol back to North Wales, asking God's blessing on 'the inhabitants of lovely Gwynedd.' It seems unlikely that its recipients would have had the stamina to sing it all, even if they had had the opportunity and the courage. Nevertheless it was doubtless passed from hand to hand, and copied by those who shared its author's religious and political sympathies. The same was probably true of his satirical 'round the houses' carol. His poems gave a boost to a people who felt oppressed by an alien ruler who despised their customs and beliefs. However Cromwell's days were already numbered, while Wales was on the threshold of the post-Restoration golden age of carol writing in which the genius of Huw Morys and Edward Morus would shine forth.

On-line Shop

All our books can be purchased
from our website

• Walking and Mountaineering
• Regions of Wales/Local Guides
• Maritime Wales
•Welsh Heritage and Culture
• Art and Photography
• Welsh History and Myths
• Children's Books
* Many books are available
at discounted prices *

www.carreg-gwalch.com

Also of interest ....

Visit our website for further information:
www.carreg-gwalch.com

Orders can be placed on our
On-line Shop

Also of interest ....

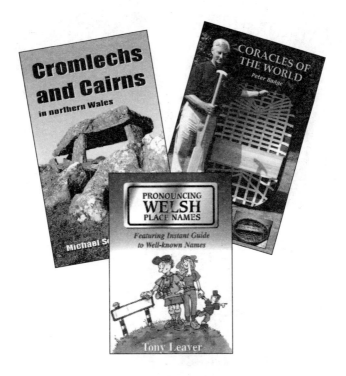

Visit our website for further information:
www.carreg-gwalch.com

Orders can be placed on our
On-line Shop